T0344735

DOSTOEVSKY'S

THE DEVILS

A Critical Companion

Edited by W. J. Leatherbarrow

Northwestern University Press

The American Association of Teachers

of Slavic and East European Languages

Northwestern University Press

Evanston, Illinois 60208-4210

Copyright © 1999 by Northwestern University Press. Published 1999.

All rights reserved.

Printed in the United States of America

ISBN 0-8101-1444-5

Library of Congress Cataloging-in-Publication Data

Dostoevsky's The devils : a critical companion / edited by W. J.

Leatherbarrow.

    p.   cm.

Includes bibliographical references.

ISBN 0-8101-1444-5 (paper)

   1. Dostoyevsky, Fyodor, 1821-1881. Besy. I. Leatherbarrow,

William J.

PG3325.B63D67   1999

891.73'3—dc21   99-27505

                                          CIP

Contents

Acknowledgments, vii
A Note on Transliteration, ix

I. INTRODUCTION

The Devils in the Context of Dostoevsky's Life
and Works, 3
    W. J. Leatherbarrow

II. CRITICISM

The Devils in the Context of Contemporary Russian
Thought and Politics, 63
    D. C. Offord

The Narrator and Narrative Technique
in Dostoevsky's *The Devils*, 100
    M. V. Jones

Dostoevsky's *The Devils:* The Role
of Stepan Trofimovich Verkhovensky, 119
    R. M. Davison

III. PRIMARY SOURCES

Extracts from Dostoevsky's Correspondence Relating
to *The Devils*, 137

IV. SELECT BIBLIOGRAPHY, 155

Contributors, 165

Acknowledgments

I am grateful to Malcolm Jones and Derek Offord for providing new essays especially for this volume, as well as for their helpful comments on draft versions of my own introduction. The essay by Roy Davison was originally published in *Forum for Modern Language Studies* 16 (1980): 109–19, and I am grateful to the publishers and to Oxford University Press for permission to reprint.

In my work on the introduction I have drawn on some material originally published in my monograph *Fedor Dostoevsky* (Boston: G. K. Hall, 1981).

A Note on Transliteration

In the bibliography and notes, and in linguistic citations, Russian words, names, titles, and phrases are transcribed from the Cyrillic according to the Library of Congress transliteration system. Elsewhere, a less formal system operates, particularly for proper names, which are given in their more familiar forms, e.g., Peter Verkhovensky, rather than Petr Verkhovenskii.

I   INTRODUCTION

The Devils in the Context of Dostoevsky's Life and Works

W. J. LEATHERBARROW

When Fedor Mikhailovich Dostoevsky started work on *The Devils* (also known in English as *The Possessed*) late in 1869, he was in his forty-eighth year and an established author with two outstanding novels, *Crime and Punishment* and *The Idiot*, already to his credit, as well as several other substantial works. His career had begun dramatically in 1845, when his sentimental novel in letters, *Poor Folk*, was brought to the attention of Vissarion Belinsky (1811–1848), Russia's leading literary critic and a touchstone for all that was progressive in social and intellectual life. Belinsky was deeply moved by the insight and apparent sympathy with which the young author had probed the emotional and psychological world of his characters, and by what he saw as a progressive humanism and alertness to social injustice underpinning Dostoevsky's depiction of the lower reaches of Russian society. He predicted a great future for the author and took him under his wing, but the critic was disappointed and puzzled by the works with which Dostoevsky followed his initial success. Novellas like *The Double* (1846) and *The Landlady* (1847) seemed less focused on social problems and more concerned with the exploration of abnormal psychology and the confusion of the worlds of reality and fantasy. Belinsky dismissed them as "terrible rubbish," and, by the time of his death in 1848, he and his young protégé were almost totally estranged.

The reader of *The Devils* will find much that is instructive in those aspects of Dostoevsky's art that provoked disagreement with Belinsky in the 1840s. First, Dostoevsky's works were never, not even at that time, primarily focused outward onto the social and political conditions that gave rise to social inequality. Thus, he could never have been the social novelist with a progressive, reforming agenda that Belinsky wished him to be on the strength of his reading of *Poor Folk*. Even in that work Dostoevsky's account of poverty, degradation, and inequality is very much secondary to analysis of the inner complexity of even the most socially insignificant individuals, as they struggle to reconcile their personal aspirations with the constraints imposed by their lowly status. This inward focus is even more evident in *The Double*, where the account of the hero's descent into madness reveals both Dostoevsky's ability to dramatize abnormal psychology and his profound understanding of the complexities of human nature. In an undated comment in his notebooks, toward the end of his life, Dostoevsky observed: "They call me a psychologist. This is not true. I am merely a realist in a higher sense, that is, I depict all the depths of the human soul."[1] It was this adoption of a "higher" realism, with its emphasis on the depths of individual human experience, that lay at the heart of Dostoevsky's estrangement from Belinsky, who fought instead for the emergence of a "natural school" of Russian literature that would foreground man's social experiences and promote the desire for social change.

Second, even in his earliest works, Dostoevsky, unlike Belinsky, recognized the value of the kind of art that skirts the irrational, and his own "higher realism" is one in which the depiction of the familiar and the everyday is enlarged by the encroachment of the apparently fantastic and grotesque. Later, in a letter dated 26 February 1869, Dostoevsky wrote to his friend N. N. Strakhov: "I have my own view of reality (in art), and that which most people call almost fantastic and exceptional is sometimes for me the very essence of the real. Everyday phenomena and a conventional view of them, in my opinion, not only fall short of realism, but are even its opposite" (29/i:19). Admittedly, Dostoevsky was writing to Strakhov about *The Idiot*, the serialization of which had recently finished in *The Russian Herald*, but the reader will note that this was also the year in which the novelist's creative thoughts turned to what would become *The Devils*. Indeed, in the final text of that novel Dostoevsky allows his character Stepan Trofimovich Verkhovensky to articulate much the same view: "My friend, real truth is never true-to-life, did you know that? In order to make the truth true-to-life you really have to stir a bit of falsehood into it" (10:172). The importance of this for an understanding of the "realism" of *The Devils* is something to which we shall return, for this is a work that combines, within its novelistic form, satire of current political realia and elements drawn from gothic and romantic literature, and that transcends the merely contemporary and everyday in order to develop a compelling mythical drama of damnation and redemption.

Finally, Belinsky, in his preoccupation with the social implications of Dostoevsky's early works, paid scant attention to the formal and narrative devices employed in them. The use of the epistolary form in *Poor Folk* was clearly designed to facilitate access to the inner world of the two main characters and to promote psychological analysis. But Dostoevsky's adoption of what was by then an outmoded narrative form served a further, artistically even more important purpose: It removed from the act of reading the mediating function of the third-person narrator. Instead of receiving information via an omniscient narrator, who is able to pattern, clarify, and objectify the experience of the fictional characters, the reader of *Poor Folk* is allowed direct and unmodified access to the subjective consciousnesses of hero and heroine. The result is that gaps and uncertainties in the hero's perception or comprehension result in gaps and uncertainties in the narrative itself, for there is no "author" to fill such gaps for us. The act of reading thus becomes unstable and uncertain but also highly creative, since readers must constantly remind themselves of the limitations of the narrative source. This technique is developed beyond the conventions of the epistolary form in works like *The Double* and *The Landlady*, both of which appear to employ third-person narrators but in which the narrator is limited to a stream-of-consciousness reporting of the hero's experience. *The Devils* takes the process of destabilizing narrative further still through its use of a narrator-chronicler who participates in the events he describes and whose trustworthiness is compromised by his closeness to the action and by his intellectual limitations. This, too, is something to which we must return.[2]

Dostoevsky's works of the 1840s thus display, in embryonic form, certain artistic characteristics of his later novels, including *The Devils*. What has not yet emerged from the discussion so far are the origins of that novel's ferociously reactionary political stance and of its biting indictment of socialism and the Russian revolutionary movement. Yet this, too, is to be found in Dostoevsky's experiences in the 1840s. In the spring of 1847 the author began to attend the Friday evening meetings of a discussion circle organized by Mikhail Petrashevsky, an eccentric scholar-socialist whom he had met the previous year. Such circles had become a characteristic feature of Russian intellectual life in the 1830s and 1840s, when the repressive regime of Tsar Nicholas I, still smarting after the abortive Decembrist revolt of 1825, had driven much intellectual and political activity underground, and when, for many would-be reformers, talk became a substitute for action and the only alternative to inertia. The talk at Petrashevsky's was of socialism, and discussion centered on the works of European utopian socialists such as Proudhon, Saint-Simon, Louis Blanc, Fourier, and Pierre Leroux. In the heady mix of liberty, equality, and fraternity advocated by such mentors, the young Dostoevsky found a secular and more tangible equivalent to the deeply held Orthodox Christian convictions he had acquired as a child. He was drawn ever deeper into the activities of the Petrashevsky circle, activities that eventually transcended abstract discussion and became conspiratorial. A key role in Dostoevsky's growing involvement was played by Nikolai Speshnev, a charismatic, enigmatic, and attractive figure in the Byronic mold, whose willpower and manipulative personality drew in the naive young writer. It is not hard to see in Speshnev an early model for the mysterious figure of Nikolai Stavrogin, the hero of *The Devils*.

In April 1849 the Petrashevsky circle was broken up by the tsarist police, and its ringleaders, including Dostoevsky, were arrested and charged with subversion. At the trial, which began the following month and ended in November, Dostoevsky and the other leading conspirators were found guilty and sentenced to death by firing squad. In a cruel charade, contrived by Tsar Nicholas himself, the sentence was commuted at the very last moment, as the condemned faced execution, to hard labor followed by Siberian exile. Dostoevsky served four years in the Omsk penal colony and a further period in the ranks. He did not return to St. Petersburg until December 1859. His Siberian experiences proved to be a decisive turning point in his development both as man and artist. It was there, as he later acknowledged, that he first discovered the Russian people (*narod*) and developed a respect for the simple Russian man, uncontaminated by Western European cultural influences, on which he was to base the Russophile nationalism and populism of his later writings. This was to become a major theme in *The Devils*. The experience of the prison camp also allowed Dostoevsky a profound insight into the criminal mind, which in turn served to disabuse him of his earlier utopianism, to strip him of whatever political idealism remained from his experience of the Petrashevsky circle, and to convince him that reason was powerless to reclaim the depraved human soul and that man's future happiness depended on his complete moral and spiritual regeneration, not on the political designs of revolutionaries and socialists. As he later wrote to S. D. Ianovsky (4 February 1872): "[I was] a man sick *with a spiritual illness* (I admit that now) before my journey to Siberia, where I was cured" (29/i:229). This rethinking of his past revolutionary associations supports the whole structure of Dostoevsky's vehement antiradicalism in *The Devils*, although it was to be consolidated by further developments he witnessed in Russian political life after his return from exile. In the early chapters of *The Devils*, which deal with the past history of Stepan Trofimovich Verkhovensky, himself a liberal Westernizer of the 1840s, Dostoevsky provides an ironic account of the activities of the "progressive" intelligentsia of his own generation, even including a passing mention of the discovery and arrest of "some sort of huge, *unnatural* society, opposed to the state, consisting of about thirteen people, and which had practically shaken the whole edifice" (10:9). The italics are mine, for they emphasize that by this time Dostoevsky had come to regard such political activity as a destructive and alien intruder in the organism of Russian life.

If Dostoevsky resumed his career in 1860 as a reformed man and a writer whose mission was now a religious one in its dedication to spiritual, rather than political transformation, the Russia he found on his return was equally radically changed. Nicholas I had died in 1855, soon after the debacle of the Crimean War, and his oppressive, stagnant regime had been swept away in a sudden reinvigoration of intellectual life and by a demand for the wholesale modernization of Russian society. The new tsar, Alexander II, himself a reformer, went some way to meeting such demands, signing in 1861 an edict proclaiming the emancipation of the serfs, that overwhelming majority of the Russian population who had hitherto lived in a state of slavery, deprived of even the most basic human rights. This "paper emancipation" largely satisfied the moderate liberal wing of the intelligentsia with its guarantee of legal freedom for the peasant, but in its failure to provide the economic means that would allow the realization of that freedom, it served only to radicalize many intellectuals, particularly those of the younger generation or from non-noble backgrounds. The result was the emergence of an intense factionalism in Russian intellectual and political life. The new generation of radical "men of the sixties" rallied around the journal *The Contemporary*, where their writings displayed a hard-headed realism, an intolerance of half-hearted measures, a scornful dismissal of the humane and romantic liberalism of the older generation of reformers, a rejection of the tsarist order, and a shrill demand that society be reconstructed on rational and scientific foundations. The novelist Ivan Turgenev offered a penetrating portrait of the "new man" in the figure of Bazarov in his novel *Fathers and Sons* (1862), and the term *nihilism* (from the Latin *nihil* – nothing) was quickly, and unfairly, coined to describe the new generation's apparent lack of beliefs and its rejection of past values. Social tensions sharpened in 1861–62 with the creation of a revolutionary party Land and Liberty, outbreaks of incendiarism in the capital, the closure of *The Contemporary*, and the arrest of leading radicals. As the 1860s unfolded, sections of the radical intelligentsia turned increasingly to terrorist acts, culminating in an unsuccessful attempt on the tsar's life by the student Dmitry Karakozov in 1866.

It was against this background of factionalism and social disorder that Dostoevsky sought to resume his literary career. Anxious to contribute his own word to the furious debates of the age, he started the journal *Time* in 1861 with his brother Mikhail. The journal's position on major issues reflected the perspectives Dostoevsky had acquired following his Siberian experiences. It attempted to steer a moderate course of national reconciliation through the disputes and class divisions of the early 1860s. Its basic premise was that beneath the tensions of the age, the essential and healing elements of Russian national and religious life were kept alive by the ordinary Russian peasant, and that the intellectual classes, torn from these roots by the aping of Western European influences, must seek to recapture their identity by returning to the "soil" of native Russia. *Time* was closed by the censor in 1863, but its line was broadly pursued by Dostoevsky's second journalistic venture *The Epoch*, until that periodical collapsed under financial pressures in 1865.

Dostoevsky's early contributions to *Time* show that his attitude to the new generation of radicals was initially one of tolerance and curiosity, but as the decade unfolded and the social and political consequences of "nihilism" began to emerge, the writer became increasingly hostile. In particular, he took issue with the views expressed by the intellectual leader of the Russian radicals, Nikolai Chernyshevsky (1828–1889), whose writings expressed the new materialism in their affirmation that human nature lacked a spiritual dimension, that man's behavior was determined solely by reason and self-interest, and that moral and social systems should be erected on the utilitarian and "scientific" principle of the greatest good of the greatest number. For Dostoevsky, such ideas, drawn from the poisoned well of secular European thought, were morally destructive, un-Russian, and symptomatic of the spiritual bankruptcy of a Russian intellectual class alienated from the wellsprings of Russian Christian tradition.

Dostoevsky's views and his repudiation of nihilist premises were not confined to his journalism but spilled over to color his fictional works, too. Indeed, his two greatest novels of the mid-1860s were originally conceived as polemical engagements with the ideas of Chernyshevsky, although it is true to say that both works outgrew such narrowly ideological beginnings. *Notes from Underground* (1864) challenges in incisive philosophical and psychological detail Chernyshevsky's insistence on the rationality of man, and questions the role of self-interest and utility in the springs of human behavior. Its hero cultivates perversity and whim, even to the extent of acting against his own well-being, and the extent to which he is prepared to exercise his own egoism and will to power gives the lie to any belief that a perfect society might be constructed on the basis of imperfect individuals. He remains to the end an unsightly blot on the radical blueprint for social order, although Dostoevsky did intend to show that this fallen soul could be reclaimed by spiritual transfiguration. His design was thwarted, however, by the censor's pencil, and the Underground Man remains a potent symbol of man's exclusion from paradise, posturing impotently in the vacuum of his own meaningless freedom. "That swine of a censor," Dostoevsky wrote to his brother in March 1864. "The passages where I jeered at everything and sometimes blasphemed *for form's sake* he let through, but he suppressed the place where from all this I deduced the need for faith and for Christ" (28/ii:73).

Crime and Punishment (1866) is erected on the same twin pillars of antinihilism and the affirmation of faith. Its hero Raskolnikov, in enacting the utilitarian moral and social formulas of the men of the sixties, discovers that they lead not to personal and social enlightenment and emancipation but to murder and despair. The theoretician-murderer finds himself unable to live with a crime that his reason condones. He discovers not only the limitations of abstractly conceived ethics but also his own humanity and spirituality. Aided by the Christian compassion of the prostitute Sonia, he learns how the truth is to be found in his own soul rather than in rational systems, and he discovers in the novel's epilogue the religious epiphany denied the hero of *Notes from Underground*. Dostoevsky's advocacy of spiritual rather than social renewal, his insistence that a harmonious social order can only be erected on the basis of good men and not on the basis of rational ideologies and institutions, also underlies *The Idiot* (1868), and it determines the conception of its hero Prince Myshkin. This novel is profoundly ambiguous, and in it Dostoevsky's artistry and sense of reality allow him to resist the temptation to utopian oversimplification. Myshkin may well be the "positively good man," but he is also a failure, for he lives in a godless age and he is open to corruption in it. He is presented as a Christlike figure, flawed by human weaknesses and adrift in a Russia beset by materialism, greed, and self-interest. If Dostoevsky's sense of artistic truth insisted that his hero must fail, then this in no way detracted from the value of the ideals he imperfectly embodied.

This brief review of Dostoevsky's attitudes and major works before the writing of *The Devils* serves to show how that novel, so often regarded as an ill-tempered departure by its author into political satire, a departure driven more by malice than by inspiration, was in fact a natural and significant new stage in the organic process of his spiritual, ideological, and artistic evolution. Its grotesque caricature of the Russian revolutionary movement was no mere heated response to the events of the day but drew on a securely established seam of antinihilism; its affirmation of the emptiness of an existence without God derived from convictions Dostoevsky had formed much earlier; and its exposure of the spiritual bankruptcy of educated Russians alienated from their native roots was founded on a view of Western Europe that already lay at the very heart of Dostoevsky's thought.

The Ideological Background to *The Devils*

Dostoevsky's work on *The Devils* began in Dresden, in the midst of a protracted and unhappy period spent in Western Europe. He had left Russia in the spring of 1867, only weeks after his marriage to Anna Grigorevna Snitkina, the young stenographer he had hired the previous year to allow him to complete on time his short novel *The Gambler*. The European trip was planned partly as a honeymoon and partly as a way of escaping the increasingly insistent demands of Dostoevsky's creditors. In both respects it was seen as a short-term measure, but Dostoevsky's inability to achieve the financial security that would allow him to pay off his debts and return home, a problem compounded by his mania for roulette, conspired to keep him abroad until July 1871, about halfway through the writing of *The Devils*. This sojourn abroad, during which the couple lived in Germany, Switzerland, and Italy, was not without its rewards. Dostoevsky was profoundly struck by the art treasures of Western Europe, particularly in Basle, where he saw Hans Holbein's painting *Christ in the Tomb*, which figures so large in *The Idiot*, and in the Royal Picture Gallery in Dresden, where Claude Lorrain's *Acis and Galatea* provided the novelist with an image of the Golden Age which he was to incorporate into Stavrogin's vision of paradise lost in *The Devils*. But such distractions did little to alleviate Dostoevsky's unhappiness, his longing for Russia, and his growing despair at what he saw as the spiritual emptiness of European civilization. "If only you knew," he wrote to his friend Apollon Maikov at the end of 1870, "what a profound revulsion Europe has aroused in me in these past four years, to the point of hatred. My God, what prejudices we Russians have about Europe!" (29/i:161). A year earlier he had written to his niece Sofia Ivanova, saying: "I remember Russia and think about her every day, to the point of intoxication. I long to return as soon as possible, whatever it might cost" (29/i:88). He also felt that residence abroad was prejudicial to him as an artist and that it sapped his creative abilities: "It is absolutely essential that I return to Russia. Here I shall soon lose even the possibility of writing, since I don't have at hand the material that you always need for it, that is Russian reality (which furnishes ideas) and the Russian people" (letter to S. Ivanova, 25 January 1869, in 29/i:11).

Dostoevsky's unhappiness and homesickness were, if anything, augmented rather than diminished by the presence in Dresden of a large Russian émigré community. His distaste for Europe and Europeans was exceeded only by the contempt he nurtured for those who had voluntarily turned their back on Russia in pursuit of some seductive European grail. That Dostoevsky refused to seek out the company of his fellow émigrés hints at his feelings, but his views are most lucidly expressed through the character of Mrs. Epanchina in *The Idiot*, who provides that novel's revealingly anti-Western conclusion: "It's time we all came to our senses. And all this, all this life abroad, all this Europe of yours, it's all just a delusion, and all of us abroad are just a delusion . . . Mark my words, you'll see for yourself!" (8:510). It was the novelist Ivan Turgenev who provided the peg on which Dostoevsky was able to hang his hatred for Russians who had implicitly renounced their nationality. He had met and quarrelled with Turgenev in Baden in 1867, and the two remained bitter foes until shortly before Dostoevsky's death. Dostoevsky disliked Turgenev's affectations and his condescendingly aristocratic manner; he envied him the financial security that allowed him to write without the hardships that attended the composition of his own novels; but above all he rejected Turgenev's liberal posturing, the shameless manner in which he courted the admiration of the younger generation, and his unquestioning preference for things European over indigenous Russian culture. Turgenev had spent much of his life in the West, where he moved easily among European literati. By conviction he was a Westernizer, a term first applied in the 1840s to those intellectuals who adopted a pro-European position and who argued that Russia's destiny lay in emulation of Western civilization, as distinct from the Slavophiles who argued the uniqueness and superiority of native Russian cultural principles. Turgenev's Westernism took the form of a preference for the French language over Russian, an admiration for the liberalism and individualism enshrined in the European political tradition, and a tendency to consign his native land to the historical dustbin. Such ideas were anathema to Dostoevsky, who had originally admired Turgenev's *Fathers and Sons* but who came to see its author as "the most written-out of all written-out Russian writers" (29/i:129), a man whose talent had drained away along with his knowledge of

Russia. In *The Devils*, of course, Turgenev is the barely concealed prototype for the "great novelist" Karmazinov, and the clash of Westernizer and Slavophile ideologies is dramatized in the relations between Kirillov and Shatov, who live in the same house but look in opposite directions in their pursuit of meaning. But the notebooks for that novel also indicate that the character of Stavrogin (referred to in earlier drafts as the Prince) was designed in part to suggest what Dostoevsky saw as the tragedy of the Europeanized Russian, whose loss of nationality translates into loss of all purpose and meaning in his life. In a passage dated 15 March 1870, we read:

> The Prince is a man who is becoming bored. A product of the age in Russia. He acts haughtily and is capable of relying only on himself, i.e., turning away from the gentry, the Westernizers, the nihilists . . . (but the question remains for him: what in effect is he? For him the answer is: *nothing*). He has great intelligence, enough to realize that he is indeed not a Russian. He makes do with the thought that *he has no need to be Russian*, but when he is confronted with the absurdity of what he has said, he takes refuge in the phrase that he is capable of relying only on himself. . . . Shatov shows him that he is incapable of love because he is a universal man (*obshchechelovek*), and the capacity to love is granted only to those who possess nationality. . . . Author's idea: to present a man who has acknowledged that he lacks native soil. (11:134–35)

It is clear from the foregoing that Dostoevsky's views on Western Europe, Russia, and the relationship of nationality to personality are interrelated and form a key part of the ideological axis on which *The Devils* turns. As such they deserve more detailed discussion. These ideas began to emerge after Dostoevsky's Siberian experiences had revealed the hollowness of his previous position; but they took a more coherent shape as the result of the writer's first visit to Europe in 1862, during which he spent time in Germany, France, England, Switzerland, and Italy. The consequences for his ideological reorientation of the impressions gleaned while abroad are described in his

Winter Notes on Summer Impressions (1863). As Joseph Frank has observed, this collection of essays and travel notes is no mere account of Dostoevsky's journey, but rather an "occasion to explore the whole tangled history of the relationship between educated Russians and European culture."[3] On one level, the work provides an ironic inversion of the respect traditionally shown by educated Russians for the cultural and historical achievements of Europe, that "land of sacred wonders" (5:47), as well as a crudely xenophobic parade of the national characteristics of the Europeans Dostoevsky had encountered. Thus Switzerland is dismissed as depressing and dull, the women of Dresden are described as repulsive, and the French are lampooned for their love of empty eloquence and bourgeois order. But on a deeper level, Dostoevsky's critical attitude betrays his conviction that Western European civilization is founded on a catastrophic social defect that presages imminent cultural collapse. In an important passage where he describes the sharp social contrasts he had observed in London, Dostoevsky writes: "But all the same, here, too, there is that persistent, smouldering, and already chronic struggle: the fight to the death between the individuality common to Western man and the necessity somehow or other to live together in harmony, to form a community" (5:69). This appears to be suggesting that European society lacked the organic unity that would allow the reconciliation of social and individual impulses. Instead, it offered only a stark choice between two options, each unacceptable to Dostoevsky: either the pursuit of personal freedom at the expense of social order or the sacrifice of the individual to political, economic, or social necessity. Later, in *Winter Notes,* in a passage discussing the socialist slogan of *liberté, égalité, fraternité,* Dostoevsky gives this idea an inflection derived from his own convictions, grounded in the Orthodox ideal of brotherhood in Christ. The passage is important enough for our purposes to be quoted in full:

Western man speaks of brotherhood as the great moving idea of humanity, and he fails to realize that brotherhood cannot be achieved where it does not exist in reality. What is to be done?

Brotherhood must be brought about at all costs. But it turns out that it is impossible to bring about brotherhood, for it brings itself about, it manifests itself, and it is to be found naturally. But in the French nature, indeed in the Western European nature in general, brotherhood is not present. Instead we find the personal principle, the principle of the isolated individual, of intense self-preservation, self-affirmation, and self-determination in one's own individual ego, and the opposition of that ego to the whole of nature and all other people in the form of an autonomous, self-justifying principle claiming equal value and status with everything outside it. From such opposition brotherhood cannot come. Why? Because in brotherhood, in real brotherhood, it is not the autonomous personality, not the ego, that should be concerned about its right to equal value and status with *all the rest*; instead, without being asked, *all the rest* should have come to that ego, to that individual claiming its rights, and proclaimed it equal to everything else in the world. Moreover, that very same rebellious and demanding personality should before anything else have sacrificed all its ego, the whole of itself, to society. Not only should it not have demanded its own rights, but, on the contrary, it should have surrendered those rights to society unconditionally. But the Western European personality is not used to such a state of affairs: it makes its demands by force, it demands its rights, it wants its share – and so you don't get brotherhood. Of course, this can all be changed, can it not? But such change takes thousands of years to come about, for such ideas must first become part of our flesh and blood if they are to become real. (5:79)

This reveals the core of Dostoevsky's misgivings about the West and the reasons for his lack of faith in the solutions proposed by European social thinkers: Those solutions were abstractions plucked from the air, and they took no account of the moral inability of European man to translate them into reality, an inability clearly demonstrated by the terror and violence into which the French Revolution had dissolved. This moral failing in turn derived, in

Dostoevsky's view, from the essentially *secular* nature of European civilization, founded on a religion – Catholicism – which had traded in the kingdom of God in exchange for the temporal authority of the Vatican and had thus replaced a truly Christian moral order, based on self-sacrifice and cooperation, with one based on self-interest and coercion. No political tinkering by well-meaning social reformers could mask this flaw in the very foundations of European society:

> There's no way anything can be done, for it is essential that it should have come about itself, that it should be part of the natural make-up. It should unconsciously form part of the nature of the whole race. In a word, for the principle of fraternal love to exist, it is first necessary to love. The race itself must be drawn instinctively toward brotherhood, toward community and agreement, and it must be drawn in spite of all the nation's sufferings down the ages, in spite of the barbaric crudeness and ignorance which might have taken root in the nation, in spite of centuries of slavery and the incursion of outsiders. (5:80)

The details Dostoevsky gives of this ideal race, which embodies the collective principle despite its backwardness, slavery, and history of foreign invasion, make it clear that he is writing about Russia, or, rather, about that section of the Russian nation that has not been corrupted by the malign influence of the West – the peasantry, with its communal landholding, its collective decision making in the *mir*, or village council, and its customs rooted in Orthodox tradition. We see here how close Dostoevsky's views were to classical Slavophilism. The early Slavophiles, such as Aleksei Khomiakov, Ivan Kireevsky, and Konstantin Aksakov, had argued that Russia, as the result of its historical isolation from Western Europe and its adoption of Orthodox Christianity instead of Roman Catholicism, had evolved a social order based on entirely different principles to those found in the West. This social order emphasized freedom rather than necessity, communality rather than individuality, and cooperation rather than confrontation. The freedom it embodied was not, of course, the abstract, illusory, and meaningless personal and political freedom for which the individual struggled in the West, but the true moral freedom found when the individual is absorbed in the body of the community, like a cell in a living organism. This idealized view of Russian society was complemented by an equally romantic view of its political structures. For the Slavophiles, the principles of tsarist rule were completely different from those which had underpinned autocracy in the West. The Russian tsar did not wield the despotic, unlimited power exercised against the people by European emperors and kings; instead, he ruled as a benevolent, paternal figure whose administration of state affairs spared the people from involvement in political life. Freedom was thus understood by the Slavophiles as freedom *from* politics, not as the greater participation of the people in political decision making advocated by European democratic thought. Russian society was thus structured on the principle of mutual noninterference of state and people in each other's affairs and was animated by mutual respect and the free expression of public opinion.[4]

This uniquely happy social order had, in the view of the Slavophiles, been corrupted by the process of the Westernization of Russia begun by Peter the Great and continued by Catherine the Great. Peter's imposition of European institutions, traditions, and attitudes on the Russian people, along with Catherine's wholesale adoption of European culture, had marked an intrusion by the state into the affairs of the people. The people had responded by insisting on greater participation in the affairs of the tsar, and the result had been the breakdown of the traditional patriarchal order, the setting of class against class, and the fragmentation of society into mutually hostile groups. Dostoevsky suggests his sympathy with such a view of the Petrine reforms when, in the notebooks to *The Devils*, he has Shatov say:

> You'll see, the moment we grasp our own nationality, learning and art will appear in our country. If only we would be what we are and become ourselves. A paralysis has descended over us from the time of the Petrine reforms. Yes, we gained half a kopeck. That

much is true, we gained half a brass kopeck, and half a brass kopeck is no mean thing. You can't create it out of nothing. Half a brass kopeck is incomparably better than nothing at all. The trouble is for that half-kopeck we so wanted, we paid out five of our rubles – real silver rubles of the kind you don't find anymore. What is more, they were our last. We gave up everything we had. (11:137–38)

Not quite everything, for the Westernization of Russia was largely confined to the educated classes. The *narod* was to all intents and purposes untouched by its processes and effects. Locked still in the traditions of Russia's pre-Petrine past, it kept alive for both the Slavophiles and Dostoevsky the essential Russian nationality on which the future rested. This point is effectively dramatized in a scene in *The Devils*, which suggests just how deeply such ideas had penetrated the fabric of the novel. Book 2, chapter 10, describes the "revolt" of the workers at the Shpigulin factory and the attempts of the governor, von Lembke, to disperse the crowd by force. The irony of the scene lies in the fact that the revolt is no such thing: It is a peaceful and orderly attempt by the people to petition their superiors, an expression of popular opinion of the sort enshrined in traditional Russian social relations. "In my opinion," writes the narrator, "there was no need for a revolt in this instance, or even for specially elected workers, for this was an ancient, historical means of resolving grievances. The Russian people have, from time immemorial, loved to have a chat with 'the general himself,' just for the satisfaction of it and regardless of the outcome." Moreover, even if the radicals had attempted to incite these workers, nothing would have come of it: "As far as revolt is concerned, then even if the factory workers had understood anything of the propaganda, they would probably have stopped listening at once, regarding it as stupid and entirely inappropriate" (10:336). Von Lembke is, however, as his name suggests, a representative of that alien administrative structure which Peter the Great had imported into Russian life and which had displaced the traditional bonds between authority and people. He sees only conspiracy and rebelliousness in the actions of the workers, and force is the only response he knows. The image of him riding astride his horse-drawn carriage, "drawn up to his full height, holding onto a strap attached for that purpose to the side, and extending his right arm out into space, just like a monument" (10:336), is surely designed to recall in the reader's mind Falconet's famous statue of Peter the Great in St. Petersburg. Such cultural "signs" embedded in this incident enlarge a superficially humorous account of von Lembke's administrative failings into a minor metaphor for the historico-cultural divisions played out in a major key elsewhere in the novel.

National identity is thus central to Dostoevsky's conception of both the fully developed Russian man and the proper Russian social order, yet this was a truth that had been lost by Russia's upper classes and by the Westernized intelligentsia of both the 1840s and the 1860s. In April 1871, while still in Dresden and working on *The Devils*, Dostoevsky wrote to Strakhov:

> Any real man of talent of any significance always ends by returning to his national feeling, by becoming national, a slavophile . . . This *law* of return to national identity applies not only to poets and literary figures, but to all other figures. Thus, finally, we can draw up a further law: If a person is really talented then he will attempt to return from the class that has blown off course back to the nation, but if he lacks real talent he not only remains in the class that has blown off course, but he becomes even more alienated from his native land and goes over to Catholicism, etc. That stinking insect Belinsky (whom you still value) was indeed weak in talent and impotent, and for that reason he cursed Russia and consciously brought it so much harm. (29/i:207–8)

Such an unflattering description of his-one time mentor is a measure of how far removed Dostoevsky had become from the Westernized intelligentsia during his work on *The Devils*. But it must be emphasized that his aversion to the Westernizers had two aspects: Not only were they trying to impose alien intellectual and social measures on Russia, they were also blind to the importance of nationality itself. Their prescription of Western remedies for what they perceived as Russia's ills betrayed the fatal *ahistoricism* of the Westernizing position, the belief that universal principles could supplant those that had emerged organically from a nation's unique historical and cultural evolution. Their attempts to apply to the living tissue of Russia abstract intellectual systems generated, like the stench of corruption, from the decaying body of Europe – an entirely different and inferior historico-cultural entity – were a measure of their alienation from their Russian past. No longer truly Russians, they had become "universal men," ghosts drifting without the anchor of national identity. Again using Belinsky as his example, Dostoevsky argued that such men wanted to "seek out the sort of nation in which not a trace of national identity remained" and that they sought to "make Russia into a *vacant* nation capable of standing at the head of the movement toward *universality*" (29/i:215). In *The Devils*, the characters of Stepan Trofimovich Verkhovensky, Peter Verkhovensky, and Nikolai Stavrogin – each a product in his way of Russia's infatuation with European culture – must be seen in the context of the views Dostoevsky held, for they were designed to illustrate stages in the alienation of the nineteenth-century Russian intelligentsia from living Russian national roots.

During his work on *The Devils* Dostoevsky found some support for his own views in the early sections of Nikolai Danilevsky's historical treatise *Russia and Europe*, which was serialized in the periodical *Dawn* during 1869 and which Dostoevsky read while in Dresden. He responded with enthusiasm to Danilevsky's assertion that Russia represented a new form of civilization based on different historical and cultural principles from those embodied in the decaying Germano-Roman civilization of the West. In a letter to his niece in March 1869, Dostoevsky refers to Danilevsky, whom he had known when both were members of the Petrashevsky circle, as "a most remarkable man . . . a one-time socialist and Fourierist . . . who has now returned as a completely national Russian man" (29/i:25). To Maikov he had earlier written: "I have heard nothing of Danilevsky since 1849, but I thought about him at times. I remember what a fanatical Fourierist he was. And now he returns from Fourierism to Russia, becomes Russian once more, and loves his native soil again, along with its essence! That's the sign of a broad nature! Turgenev went from being a Russian writer to being a German – that's the sign of a worthless nature!" (28/ii:328). Dostoevsky followed Danilevsky's theses as they unfolded on the pages of *Dawn*, but his enthusiasm was increasingly tempered by the suspicion that Danilevsky's arguments would finally founder in a shallow nationalism, without recognizing the essential ingredient in Dostoevsky's own advocacy of Russian cultural superiority. In a letter to Strakhov in March 1869, Dostoevsky writes of *Russia and Europe:* "It coincides so much with my own personal deductions and convictions that I am quite taken aback. . . . However, I am still not totally convinced that Danilevsky will show *in its full force* the ultimate essence of the Russian calling, which is to reveal to the world the Russian Christ, of whom the world is ignorant and whose origins lie in our native Orthodoxy." It was not enough merely to recognize the distinctiveness, or even the superiority, of Russian historico-cultural forms. What was important was that those forms had evolved organically from the Orthodox spirit still alive in the Russian people, and that the Russian people, having been spared the temporal delusions that had brought the Catholic West to atheism, remained the only truly Christian people. "In my view," Dostoevsky continues, "in this there lies the whole essence of our future civilizing role, and the resurrection perhaps of the whole of Europe, as well as the whole essence of our mighty future existence" (29/i:30).

It is clear from Dostoevsky's responses to Danilevsky's work that the ideas expressed by Shatov in *The Devils* are essentially Dostoevsky's own. Shatov also insists that "he who is not Orthodox cannot be a Russian," that "God is the synthetic personality of the whole people," and that "the people are the body of God" (10:197–99). But what Shatov *stands for* is rather different: He embodies the failing Dostoevsky had detected in Danilevsky's arguments. He admits to Stavrogin that the Slavophiles of today have renounced the centrality of Orthodoxy, and then demonstrates that his own stance can never transcend an empty and rhetorical nationalism, since, for all its insistence on the religious mission of the Russian people, it is ultimately unsupported by true faith in God. His admission to Stavrogin that "I *shall* believe in God" must therefore be taken in conjunction with his later response when his wife asks him whether he is a Slavophile:

> "I became a Slavophile because I could not be a Russian," he said with a crooked smile and with the effort of a man who has tried to make an inappropriate witticism that proved beyond him.
> "So you're not a Russian?"
> "No, I'm not a Russian." (10:436)

Dostoevsky's Work on *The Devils*

By October 1870 Dostoevsky was able to write to Maikov, outlining his plans for a novel clearly structured on the ideas explored in the previous section: "Take note, my dear friend: Whoever loses his people and his nationality, loses also his native faith and God. Well, if you want to know, there you have the theme of my novel. It is called *The Devils*" (29/i:145). The conception of the novel had, however, evolved and deepened considerably over the preceding year, as Dostoevsky sought to graft his most deeply held philosophical convictions onto a work that was initially envisaged as a purely propagandistic piece. A full account of the evolution of *The Devils* is not possible in an introduction of this length, and, in any case, such a task has been admirably performed already, in Russian by the editors of the Academy edition of Dostoevsky's works,[5] and in English by Edward Wasiolek and Victor Terras.[6] Here we must confine ourselves to identification of the major stages and turning points in the process of composition.

From Dostoevsky's working notebooks it is possible to ascribe the formulation of *The Devils* as a recognizably distinct entity to the beginning of 1870.[7] By the end of March of that year, he was able to write to Strakhov outlining a polemical work, to be written with some urgency, but with scant regard for lasting artistic value:

> Now, though, at the present moment, I am working on something for *The Russian Herald*. I shall finish it soon. . . . I have high hopes for the piece, but in a tendentious, rather than artistic sense. I want to utter a few ideas, even if my artistry is destroyed in the process. But I am being carried away by what has built up in my mind and heart; let it come out as merely a pamphlet, but I shall have my say. (29/i:111–12)

The dismissive, impatient manner in which Dostoevsky describes his task for *The Russian Herald* is revealing, for this was a work he felt compelled to write at a time when his real creative energies were focused on an entirely different project intended for the journal *Dawn*. Financial pressures forced this change of direction, in that he was significantly in debt to *The Russian Herald*, but he also felt the need to enter the polemical fray and speak his mind about contemporary political events in distant Russia. The terms in which he describes the work he is to lay aside are also revealing, for they suggest a project much closer to his heart:

> For me this work of mine is dearer than anything. It is one of my most cherished ideas, and I want to make a really good job of it. . . . I shall finish my work for *The Russian Herald* quickly and sit down to my novel with enjoyment. I have nurtured this idea for three years already, but hitherto I have been afraid to set about it while living abroad; for this task I wanted to be in Russia. (29/i:112)

The notebooks contain two draft plans, "Atheism" and "The Life of a Great Sinner," which reveal the nature and scale of Dostoevsky's ambitions. Following the muted reception that had greeted *The Idiot*, and ever mindful of the competition offered by Tolstoy's success with *War and Peace* as it appeared between 1866 and 1869, he felt the need to reestablish his credentials. His work on the novella *The Eternal*

Husband, completed around this time, did not satisfy him. Technically, it is one of Dostoevsky's most accomplished pieces, but his dismissive remarks about it in various letters suggest that he considered it a slight work. He longed to produce a work of real artistic and philosophical magnitude that would fire the public imagination in the way that *Crime and Punishment* had in 1866. Dostoevsky's notes for "Atheism" and later "The Life of a Great Sinner" were composed between late 1868 and early 1870. They address essentially the same project: the attempt to depict how a Russian man finds his way, after much suffering, from the depths of debauchery, atheism, and despair to a moral crisis and the regeneration of his faith. In a letter to Maikov, dated 25 March 1870, Dostoevsky explains that the project will crown his life's work and will yield a novel the size of *War and Peace:* "The main idea . . . is the same one that has tormented me consciously and unconsciously for the whole of my life – the existence of God" (29/i:117). The work was never written as such, but its basic ideas, as well as specific draft situations and characters, find their way into all Dostoevsky's subsequent major novels, including *The Devils.*

Dostoevsky was distracted from this task, however, by political events in both Europe and Russia, which he followed avidly in the newspapers. He was shaken by the Franco-Prussian war, which began in July 1870, and by the subsequent rise and destruction of the Paris Commune, occurrences that seemed to him to manifest the impending cultural collapse of Western Europe and that he regarded as ultimately posing a threat to Russia through both the increased might of Germany and the rise of the radical Left. The struggle between these two forces is ironically expressed in *The Devils* through Liamshin's piano piece, in which the *Marseillaise* and the German popular song *Mein lieber Augustin* clash in discordant, fractured harmonies (10:251–52). In Russia, meanwhile, the harvest of Western cultural and ideological influences was being reaped in growing political disorder and the emergence of revolutionary violence. "The nihilists and Westernizers need a decisive lashing," Dostoevsky wrote to Strakhov. "You're far too soft on them. With them you have to write with a whip in your hand" (29/i:113). To Maikov he wrote: "As far as nihilism is concerned, there's nothing to be said. Just wait until the whole of that upper class, which has torn itself away from the Russian soil, completely rots away" (29/i:119). The event that catalyzed Dostoevsky's increasing aversion to the Russian radicals was the murder, in November 1869, of the young student Ivanov at the hands of a group of conspirators led by Sergei Nechaev. The incident also furnished Dostoevsky with the basic plot outline for his "pamphlet-novel." The "Nechaev affair," as it quickly became known, was one of the most intriguing and scandalous episodes in the history of the nineteenth-century radical movement, combining as it did naivety and deceit, pathos and the absurd, low comedy and high tragedy. Its appeal for Dostoevsky was surely centered on its emblematic potential, for not only did it express his deepest fears about radical Russian youth, it also possessed, in the way it crossed the boundaries between the traditional categories mentioned above, the ability of what Bakhtin has termed the *carnivalesque* to squeeze new meaning from the breakdown of such established categories.[8] The details of the affair have been well described in the critical literature,[9] and a full account is given in Derek Offord's contribution to the present volume. Here, at the risk of anticipating some details of Offord's treatment, we shall review only the aspects relevant to Dostoevsky's work on his novel. Sergei Nechaev had superficially impeccable revolutionary credentials. He claimed, untruly, that he had been arrested for participation in a student revolt, that he had escaped from the dreaded Petropavlovsky Fortress in Petersburg, scene of Dostoevsky's own incarceration in 1849, and had subsequently fled abroad. In Geneva he met Mikhail Bakunin, the notorious revolutionary and inspiration to all radical youth. Bakunin was impressed by Nechaev and helped him to organize the circulation in Russia of revolutionary pamphlets, among them a call to insurrection entitled *The Catechism of a Revolutionary*, which was almost certainly written by either Nechaev or Bakunin himself. On returning to Russia, Nechaev created a small revolutionary cell based in the Moscow Agricultural

Academy where Dostoevsky's own brother-in-law, Ivan Snitkin, was a student. He claimed the cell was one of a whole network spread throughout Russia, and that he was acting on the authority of Bakunin himself. Again, none of this was true. When Ivanov, a member of Nechaev's cell and an acquaintance of Snitkin, expressed the desire to leave the movement, Nechaev persuaded the other members that he was a risk that had to be eliminated. The murder took place on the grounds of the Agricultural Academy, and Ivanov's body was tossed into a pond. On its discovery, the members of the group were quickly rounded up and arrested, but Nechaev had already fled abroad. He was eventually extradited from Switzerland in 1872, tried the following year, and sentenced to confinement in the Petropavlovsky Fortress, where he died in 1882.

This episode, the unfolding of which Dostoevsky followed in press reports, is clearly the model on which he based the Peter Verkhovensky/Shatov plot. What is not quite so immediately evident is that Dostoevsky also used his knowledge of the revolutionary advice given in *The Catechism of a Revolutionary* in order to flesh out the details of Peter's own "revolutionary" tactics in *The Devils*, including the exploitation of the vanity of ruling officials like the von Lembkes.[10] Dostoevsky now had the "whip" with which to lash the radicals, and his pamphlet-novel quickly took shape in his notebooks. Of particular interest is an undated draft entitled "Envy," in which we can already recognize several of the final novel's major characters, including Stavrogin and Shatov, and which signals, albeit in a still muted way, the work's preoccupation with nihilism, political agitation, and revolutionary violence. The draft also makes direct reference to Nechaev by name and to the murder of Ivanov by implication (12:58, passim).

But the novel that began as a transparently political statement, and an overtly cathartic expression of Dostoevsky's disgust at the actions and opinions of the radicals, became complex and less transparent under his pen. His cherished project for "The Life of a Great Sinner" would not go away, and it began first to contaminate, and then to overwhelm, the polemical designs of the pamphlet. From the earliest notebook mention of the figure of the "Prince" it is clear that this character, later to become Stavrogin, inhabits a different world from that of the political players like Nechaev. Deeply enigmatic, he affords glimpses into moral and metaphysical depths beyond the expressive potential of a purely political pamphlet. As Wasiolek has observed, Dostoevsky was not by nature *primarily* a political writer or a commentator on current events, at least not in his novels: "Nechaev, who provoked him to have his say, is not the hero; nor is Stepan Trofimovich Verkhovensky, who starts and finishes the novel. . . . The hero is Stavrogin, who forced his way into the novel and into Dostoevsky's tormented heart. But if Stavrogin is the hero, Dostoevsky was no longer writing the pamphlet he had wanted to write."[11]

Aware that his original intention had been hopelessly compromised, Dostoevsky began afresh at the beginning of August 1870, throwing out all that had been written so far, the equivalent of 240 pages. (Dostoevsky refers to 15 galley pages – see, for example, 29/i:136.) The political dimension remains in the new plan, but it is relegated to a secondary plane in order to foreground the "great sinner," Stavrogin. This reversal of the original plot hierarchy is what allowed Dostoevsky to create a truly great novel, one that transcended the narrowly political concerns of the day. The political nihilism exhibited in the Nechaev plot is now enriched through juxtaposition with Stavrogin's primary characteristic, his *moral and spiritual nihilism. The Devils* thus becomes a multilayered exposure of nihilism in its many forms: political, philosophical, emotional, and spiritual. Its marriage of politics and philosophy swells it into the supreme antinihilist novel.

If all the above suggests that the gestation of his novel proved painful for Dostoevsky, it must also be recalled that it was conceived in an uncongenial environment and written amid difficult personal circumstances. Dostoevsky's letters and notebooks make frequent reference to his financial hardships and concern over the health of his infant daughter, as well as to the constant epileptic attacks he had to endure. "Oh, Sonia!" he wrote to his niece in August 1870, "if only you knew how hard it is to be a writer and to bear this burden. Believe me, I know for a fact that if I had two or three years in which to compose this novel, like Turgenev, Goncharov, and Tolstoy have, I would write the sort of thing they would still be talking about in a hundred years' time!" (29/i:136). A further distraction was provided by the writer's pathological addiction to gambling. In 1870 and 1871 he made trips to Homberg and Wiesbaden in order to try his luck unsuccessfully at the roulette tables. Letters written home to his wife in Dresden attest to his despair and self-loathing. In April 1871 he wrote pledging to renounce forever his passion for the tables:

> Ania, my guardian angel, something great has taken place in me: That vile fantasy which has *tormented* me for almost ten years has disappeared. For ten years . . . I have done nothing but dream of winning. I have dreamed seriously and passionately. Now it's all over and done with! This was ABSOLUTELY the last time! Believe me, Ania, my hands have been freed. I was ensnared by gambling, but now I shall think about business and no longer dream about gambling for whole nights on end, like I used to. (29/i:199)

Joseph Frank speculates interestingly about the reason behind Dostoevsky's decision to abandon his vice,[12] but he does not address the potentially more interesting issue of why Dostoevsky's gambling was confined to his periods in Western Europe. Of course, the simple answer is that Europe provided him opportunities not available in Russia, and this may well be true. But it is also possible that the lure of the European casinos, which he saw as a form of possession, had something to do with the metaphorical significance he had ascribed to gambling in his novel *The Gambler* (1866). Our point is neatly introduced by R. L. Jackson's description of Roulettenburg, the setting for that novel:

> The action of *The Gambler* takes place in a kind of no man's land or hell, Roulettenburg. As the fictitious name suggests, the city is nowhere or anywhere in Europe. The mixed French and German

components of the name suggest the *illegitimate and rootless character of the place*. This is the land of Babel, *a place without a national language or culture*. The gambling salon – the heart of Roulettenburg – is situated, symbolically, in a railway station where people are coming and going, where all is in continuous movement. Everything is in flux in this city: people, languages, currencies, values.[13]

The italics are mine, for they show that we are in the Western Europe of Dostoevsky's mind, one frequented by Russian émigrés and one from which national identity, and thus all meaning, has been abstracted. The heart of this "illegitimate" place is, significantly, a gambling casino, a temple to the contingency, blind chance, and struggle against the odds which in the West have displaced true meaning, faith, and purpose. In *The Gambler*, as Jackson puts it, "the very act of gambling becomes a conscious or unconscious affirmation of the meaninglessness of the universe,"[14] and the reality of the Russian abroad gives way to the myth of the *obshchechelovek*, "who has lost his faith and *does not dare not to believe*," whose "living juices, forces, impetuosity, and daring have gone instead into roulette" (28/ii:51), and who ekes out an empty existence in a casino in the shadow of Schlangenburg – "Snake Mountain" – with its transparently diabolical implications. What is clear from this is that the semiotic system with which Dostoevsky surrounds the act of gambling in his novel implicates that act deeply in his vision of European cultural collapse. Is it not, therefore, only to be expected that he should feel no need to gamble when in his native Russia and that such a form of demonic possession should overwhelm him during his years of desperate exile in the wilderness of Western Europe?

From "Pamphlet-Novel" to Myth

For all the metaphysical complexity brought to *The Devils* by the emergence of Stavrogin as its central figure, the finished novel retains nonetheless its overtly propagandistic purpose. That purpose and the messages it conveys are, however, now played out in a key entirely different from that Dostoevsky envisaged originally; the work goes beyond straightforward, realistic depiction of the political phenomena of its age, and its argumentation transcends directly polemical engagement with current issues on the part of the author. That is not to say that the re-thought work lacks all immediacy: Dostoevsky the publicist was unable to resist the temptation to provide a gallery of vitriolic caricatures of his ideological enemies, and prototypes for the novel's characters, major and minor, are easily identified by the historian. Clearly Peter Verkhovensky is distilled from Nechaev, and the murder of Shatov closely follows the facts of the Ivanov killing as they emerged from the trial of the conspirators.[15] Several other members of Peter's group have recognizable prototypes: The fanatical Erkel, who combines cold-blooded participation in Shatov's murder with a son's dutiful love for his mother, is drawn from what Dostoevsky learned about N. Nikolaev, a chilling assassin and Nechaev's loyal right-hand man. The ridiculous Virginsky, who encourages his wife's adultery in order to establish his credentials as a progressive thinker, takes much from a similar character created by Chernyshevsky in his novel *What Is to Be Done?* (1863), a novel that served as a source of inspiration for radical youth. Shatov is the Ivanov to Peter's Nechaev, but he is also, as we have seen, intended to represent the failure of contemporary Slavophilism to transcend empty nationalism. In this role Shatov is ideologically counterbalanced by his neighbor Kirillov, a Westernizer who has lost the ability to speak his native Russian fluently, whose atheism leads to the apotheosis of individual will, and whose sterile conception of freedom brings him inescapably to suicide.

Shigalev, the theoretician of Peter's group, advocates a view of "equality" that is arguably based on the social Darwinism advocated in the 1860s by the revolutionary populist P. N. Tkachev.[16] But in his treatment of Shigalev and his ideological system, Dostoevsky rises above the superficially satirical to offer a genuine insight into the reasons behind his rejection of socialism, and to show that *The Devils* is not just about the individual weaknesses of particular revolutionary personalities and their sympathizers but about the moral failure of revolutionary idealism itself. Dostoevsky treats Shigalev with a comparative gentleness denied the other revolutionaries in the novel. He attempts to show in Shigalev's tortured thinking the attempt of a fanatical but wholly honest revolutionary to reconcile his abstract dreams of social justice with the acknowledged reality of man's corrupt nature. Unlike Peter Verkhovensky, Shigalev is not a rogue bent on destruction for the sake of self-aggrandizement; nor is he the fool his paradoxical view of equality might lead us to believe. He is presented as an ardent social dreamer – a "Fourier," as Peter calls him – who, like Dostoevsky, has grasped the fundamental flaw in the foundations of the socialist ideal: the fact that man, at least in his agnostic European manifestation, does not possess a nature capable of true brotherhood and equality. Shigalev describes his system at the group's clandestine meeting at Virginsky's, but only Peter recognizes the real significance of his conclusions. The others ridicule him. Shigalev's starting point reflects that of all socialists: an ideal society founded on liberty, equality, and fraternity. His subsequent reasoning, however, subverts this ideal: "I have become rather confused by my own data," he confesses, "and my conclusion is a direct contradiction of the idea I start with. Starting with the ideal of unlimited freedom, I arrive at the ideal of unlimited despotism. I must add, however, that there can be no other solution to the social problem than mine" (10:311). This catastrophic reversal of Shigalev's ideals is entirely the result of his insight into human nature. He recognizes what most other social dreamers have chosen to overlook: that without God man is not by nature good; that man's immediate actions are dictated not by idealism but by egoism; and that the ideals underpinning the socialist dream are, in reality, all too readily sacrificed to personal gain and self-interest, the most characteristic manifestation of which is the will to power. Even in a "socialist" society, equality and freedom for all will be lost, as the strong force their will on the weak. Shigalev's system attempts to regulate this Darwinian acknowledgment of natural selection and the survival of the fittest by envisaging the sort of two-tier society decribed in twentieth-century anti-utopian novels like Evgenii Zamiatin's *We*,

George Orwell's *Animal Farm* and *1984*, and Aldous Huxley's *Brave New World*. For Shigalev, such a society, based on the "benevolent" despotism of the few, would guarantee happiness and equality for the many, albeit the equality of servitude. In his creation of Shigalev and "Shigalevism," Dostoevsky is drawing deeply on his own views on the nature of Western European civilization, a civilization based on self-interest in which unity can be achieved only by force. Only a truly Christian society like Russia could offer the reconciliation of freedom and brotherhood, but this solution eludes the grasp of the Westernized Shigalev.

The pivotal character in the political design of *The Devils* is not Peter Verkhovensky nor Shigalev nor indeed any other member of Peter's circle. Rather, it is Peter's father Stepan Trofimovich Verkhovensky, whose centrality is suggested in the fact that he both opens and closes the novel's action. The early chapters, along with Dostoevsky's notebooks, make it clear that Stepan Trofimovich was based on the historical figure of Timofei Granovsky (1813–1855), a professor at Moscow University whose series of public lectures in the winter of 1843–1844 secured his reputation as the leading liberal Westernizer of his generation. Indeed, throughout the notebooks and drafts, the figure that evolved into Stepan Trofimovich is referred to by that name, and in February 1870 Dostoevsky specifically requested Strakhov to send him a copy of A. V. Stankevich's book on Granovsky, saying he needed it "like the very air itself, as material absolutely necessary for work on my novel" (29/i:111). The process of composition subsequently stripped from the character of Stepan Trofimovich some, but not all, of the particular characteristics of Granovsky, so that he, too, like Peter Verkhovensky, becomes a distillation from, rather than a reflection of, historical truth. He is transformed into a generalized portrait of the liberal Westernizer of the 1840s, now in his late years. The action of *The Devils* is, of course, located in the 1860s, so that Stepan Trofimovich, as well as the generation and values he represents, have long had their day. But Dostoevsky's reason for foregrounding this historical anachronism in a novel directed against the excesses of a subsequent generation emerges from his conviction that the Westernizers of the 1840s, for all their liberal humanism, were, in fact, the progenitors of the crude and destructive nihilism of the 1860s. They first turned their back on their native Russia and its national values; they first proclaimed the superiority of Western reason to the "dark superstition" of the Russian church; and they first sought the key to social reconstruction in the doctrines of revolutionary socialists. Such a view was not new: Dostoevsky's friend Strakhov had argued the same point in an article in *Dawn* in July 1869, devoted to Stankevich's book on Granovsky. It was part of Dostoevsky's polemical design in *The Devils* to confront the liberals of his own generation with their responsibility for monsters like Nechaev, who had followed their lead and taken their beliefs to extreme but inevitable conclusions. In a letter to Strakhov in May 1871, he wrote:

> If Belinsky, Granovsky, and the rest of that riff-raff could see what is happening now, they would say: "No, that's not what we dreamed of; this is a deviation. If we wait a bit longer the light will appear, progress will reign, and mankind will reconstruct itself on healthy foundations and find happiness!" They would never agree that once you have embarked on that path, it cannot lead anywhere else. (29/i:215)

Stepan Trofimovich Verkhovensky expresses similar sentiments after his encounter with the ideas of the younger generation:

> Oh, my friends . . . you cannot imagine the sadness and anger that sieze your soul when a great idea you have long considered sacred is taken up by bunglers and dragged out into the street to fools like themselves, and you suddenly come across it in the secondhand market, unrecognizable, covered in filth, clumsily set up at an angle, without proportion, without harmony, a plaything for stupid children! No, it was different in our time; that wasn't what we strove for. (10:24)

Although a genial and humane man, Stepan Trofimovich is out of touch with Russian reality, and he comes to recognize his generation's responsibility only at the end of the novel, when he embarks on his pilgrimage to find the real Russia. Before that, however, his otherworldliness has led him into moral and political duplicity. He preaches the brotherhood of man, but abandons his own son; he advocates the abolition of serfdom, but gambles away his own serf Fedka at cards. The return of Peter and the murder of the Lebiadkins by Fedka thus assume a highly symbolic charge: They represent Dostoevsky's indictment of the generation of the 1840s for the excesses committed by the "sons."

In this juxtaposition of the two generations of the 1840s and 1860s, *The Devils* treads similar ground to that explored in Turgenev's *Fathers and Sons*. The latter work, however, had emphasized the gulf between the generations and had thus, in Dostoevsky's view, whitewashed the responsibility of the "fathers." In its implied assertion that the naive and apparently harmless generation of the 1840s had spawned a generation of monsters, *The Devils* seeks to lay the blame where it belongs, emphasizing the continuity binding both generations together in the nightmare they have unleashed on Russia.

Left-wing criticism has done its best, particularly in Soviet Russia, to disguise, overlook, or circumvent Dostoevsky's unflattering account of the Russian revolutionary movement and its actors, often pleading that the real revolutionaries – including even Nechaev himself – were in reality nothing like that, and that the way they are depicted in *The Devils* maliciously maligns their true aspirations. This is unarguably correct – Dostoevsky's political grotesques do misrepresent the real Russian revolutionaries of his time – but such criticism misses the point: Dostoevsky *knew* he was being "unfair." In October 1870 he wrote to his editor, Katkov:

Among the major events of my novel will be the well-known murder of Ivanov by Nechaev in Moscow. Let me quickly make a reservation: I knew neither Nechaev nor Ivanov nor the circumstances of that murder. I only know what I have read in the newspapers. And even if I had known them, I would not have tried to copy them. I take only the accomplished fact. It may well be that my fantasy departs in very great measure from what actually occurred and that my Peter Verkhovensky is nothing like Nechaev. But it seems to me that in my inflamed mind, imagination has created the very figure, the very type, that corresponds to such a crime. (29/i:141)

Here we see the "realist in a higher sense" sacrificing verisimilitude to mythography. The Stavrogin estate of Skvoreshniki may, or may not, resemble the park in the Moscow Agricultural Academy where Ivanov was murdered; the topography of the provincial town depicted in *The Devils* may, or may not, correspond to that of Tver, where Dostoevsky lived in 1860.[17] It matters not, for the novel transmutes both into mythical landscapes onto which metaphysical, not political, struggles are projected. Even St. Petersburg, no longer the realization of Peter the Great's dream of a window on the West through which the light of European reason would pass, looms in the novel's background as a fissure in the Russian earth through which abominations seep, a turnstile to the nether world, allowing sundry demons, great and small, to pass to and fro.

The mythography of *The Devils* is, of course, structured on this notion of demonism and demonic possession, as the novel's title and epigraphs signal. The first epigraph, taken, like the title, from a poem by Pushkin, uses the notion to evoke obliquely Dostoevsky's theme of the educated Russian classes led astray by the deceptive lure of Western Europe:

> Strike us dead, the trail has gone,
> We've lost our way, what can we do?
> A devil seems to be leading us into a field,
> And making us go around in circles.

The origins of the second epigraph, taken from St Luke's parable of the Gadarene swine, are to be found in a letter Dostoevsky wrote to Maikov on 9 October 1870. This is an important document, and extracts from it are given in section 3 of this work. Dostoevsky's bilious cast of mind is suggested right at the start, when he refers to his "vexatious" and "repulsive" work on his novel. He recalls his own political past, remembering how he was then "under the strong ferment of the mangy Russian liberalism preached by turd-eaters such as the dung-beetle Belinsky and his ilk." He proceeds to point out that "the sickness that had gripped civilized Russians was more severe than we ourselves thought, and the matter did not end with Belinsky, etc." Instead, as in the parable of the Gadarene swine, "the devils departed from the Russian man and entered into the herd of swine, that is into the Nechaevs" (29/i:145).

But Dostoevsky was to develop this motif of demons and demonism far beyond its original, purely figurative conception as a metaphor for those Russians possessed by Western ideas. His characters developed more tangible and literal symptoms of the demonic and demonic possession as the pamphlet-novel expanded into myth. Thus Stavrogin acquires the masklike face, supernatural strength, predatory instincts, and deathlike demeanor of a vampire; there is something ghoulish about the ears of Shigalev, ears that are "of an unnatural size, long, broad and thick, and somehow sticking out in a peculiar way." The narrator is further struck by the "ominous impression" Shigalev makes (10:110). Moreover, Dostoevsky emphasizes throughout the novel the peculiar irritability that seems to have seized nearly all the characters, including Stavrogin, Kirillov, Shatov, Lebiadkin, and Lizaveta. Only Maria Lebiadkina is introduced as radiating "a calm, tranquil joy" (10:114), and, significantly, she is intended to represent the native religious wisdom of the Russian *narod*.

The initial description of Peter Verkhovensky, the heart of the social disorder taking place in the novel, is particularly suggestive of the supernatural. It occurs in a chapter entitled "The Wise Serpent," and it is remarkable for its elusiveness, as though we were witnessing some intangible and diabolical mirage. It is littered with contradictions as well as the sort of evasive particles, phrases, and adjectival suffixes that dissolve semantic certainty:

At first glance it was as though he were sort of stooped and rather awkward but, however, not at all stooped and even free-and-easy. It was as though he were some sort of eccentric, but, on the other hand, we all then found his manners entirely becoming, and his conversation always to the point.

The description continues in this vein until the demon shows his distinctive trademark:

His speech was remarkably clearly articulated; his words tumbled out like large, smooth grains, always well chosen and always at your service. At first you found this appealing, but then it became repulsive, precisely because of that too clearly articulated speech and those pearls of ever-ready wisdom. Somehow or other, you began to imagine the tongue in his mouth as being surely of a special sort of shape, somehow unusually long and thin, terribly red and exceedingly sharp, with a tip that flickered constantly and involuntarily. (10:143)

We thus find ourselves suddenly in the presence not just of a Nechaev-intriguer who has arrived in town to begin his political machinations, but also of the Father of Lies, about to embark on the gathering of souls and the dissemination of destruction.

The intrusion of demonic manifestations such as these into the novel's nightmare vision of social and political reality allows Dostoevsky to develop a whole pattern of supernatural symbolism that tightly binds that vision to the apocalyptic dream-revelations of St. John in the New Testament.[18] We know for a fact that Dostoevsky kept the New Testament by his side during his Siberian years and that annotations in his own personal copy (which has survived) shed light on the process of spiritual rebirth he was then experiencing. Dostoevsky's New Testament makes it clear that the Revelation of St. John attracted proportionately more of such annotations and markings than its other books. This is perhaps owing in part to its evocative but elusive imagery, and this reminds us that we must proceed with caution in any attempt to seek the resonances of such imagery in Dostoevsky's own work. The obscure richness of the visions described in Revelation can lead to critical indigestion, and the pursuit of parallel situations in *The Devils* can result in imaginative but unfounded assertions of influence. Yet, to deny the contribution that Dostoevsky's reading of Revelation made to *The Devils* would be to overlook a suggestive aspect of that novel's poetics. We shall therefore restrict the following analysis of its apocalyptic themes and motifs to those examples that are supported either by Dostoevsky's annotations or by textual evidence in the novel itself.

Dostoevsky's consistent, as opposed to sporadic, use of apocalyptic imagery is confined to three works: *Winter Notes on Summer Impressions, The Idiot,* and *The Devils.* What these works have in common is a direct association with Dostoevsky's painful firsthand experiences of life in Western Europe: The first describes his initial impressions of the West, while the other two were largely written or conceived abroad. It is in *Winter Notes* that Dostoevsky first uses the apocalypse as a metaphor for what he had identified as the symptoms of European spiritual collapse,[19] but the climate of *The Devils* is also unmistakably apocalyptic as Dostoevsky depicts the contagion spreading to his native land. Thus, as in Revelation, the novel describes a series of catastrophes presaging the final disaster of the fête and its aftermath. Outbreaks of incendiarism and cholera in the district call to mind the scourges of fire and plague that accompany the Last Judgment. This mood is sustained by Karmazinov, who directly compares the decline of Western Europe with the fall of Babylon (10:287), and by Kirillov, who reads the apocalypse at night with Fedka the convict (10:282). Moreover, St. John's prophecies that "there will be time no more," that "there shall be no more death," and that the old heaven and earth will yield to the new are grotesquely brought to mind by Kirillov's assertion that at the moment he takes his own life and proclaims the deification of man, a new era in human existence will begin (10:187–89). This apocalyptic note is struck not just by those characters at the center of *The Devils:* The general climate of Russia in the novel is apocalyptic, and moral confusion has displaced true faith. Peter Verkhovensky describes this mood of spiritual rootlessness when he outlines to Stavrogin his plan to take advantage of it in his drive for power:

> Listen . . . Don't you realize that we are very powerful already? It's not just the ones who kill and burn . . . who belong to us. Listen, I've reckoned them all up: The teacher who laughs with his children at their God and the home that has nurtured them is already ours. The lawyer who defends an educated murderer by pleading that he is more developed than his victim and had no choice but to kill in order to get money, he, too, is already ours. Schoolboys who kill a peasant for kicks are ours. Juries who acquit criminals indiscriminately are ours. The prosecutor who trembles in court because he is not liberal enough is ours, ours. Administrators, writers – oh, there are lots and lots of us, and they don't know it themselves! On the other hand, the readiness of schoolboys and fools to obey has reached the highest point. . . . Don't you see how many we shall win over with just a few, ready-made ideas? (10:324)

Toward the end of *The Devils* Stepan Trofimovich Verkhovensky is struck by Sofia Matveevna's reading of Revelation 3:14–17: "And unto the angel of the church of the Laodiceans write: . . . I know thy works, that thou art neither cold nor hot: I would thou wert cold or hot. / So then because thou art lukewarm, and neither cold nor hot, I will spue thee out of my mouth. / Because thou sayest, I am rich, and increased with goods, and have need of nothing; and knowest not that thou art wretched, and miserable, and poor, and blind, and naked." He has recognized in these words the tragedy of his own generation's lack of conviction. The reader will also pick up the reference to Stavrogin's "lukewarm" personality. But Peter Verkhovensky intends to take advantage of a similar general moral half-heartedness in contemporary society in order to create and propagate the legend of Stavrogin the idol, a mysterious and majestic figure who will emerge from hiding and rule supreme. Here again, Dostoevsky draws his inspiration from Revelation, which in chapter 13 describes the advent of a "beast," whose name is Mystery, and who will rule over the earth with supreme power. The way is paved for this beast by a false prophet, with two horns and a dragon's tongue, who "exerciseth all the power of the first beast before him, and causeth the earth and them which dwell therein to worship the first beast" (13:12). The false prophet, moreover, "maketh fire come down from heaven on the earth in the sight of men," "deceiveth them that dwell on the earth," and causes "that as many as would not worship the image of the beast should be killed." It is difficult not to see linkages between these devils and the figures of the mysterious "wild beast" Stavrogin and the serpent-tongued deceiver Peter Verkhovensky. Peter's first appearance in the novel is when he comes on ahead to announce the arrival of Stavrogin, whom he plans to make men worship. On the night of the fête, he, too, makes fire come down to earth by organizing the incendiarism that claims the lives of Lebiadkin and his crippled sister. He practices the systematic deception of the governor's wife and the members of his own circle. And he arranges the murder of Shatov when the latter ceases to believe in his fabrications.

The apocalyptic coloring of *The Devils* is deepened when we recall the name of the Stavrogin estate, from which so much of the novel's disorder originates. Skvoreshniki is derived from *skvorechnik*, a sort of wooden bird-box in which starlings nest. This strange name, and indeed the novel's very title, acquire real significance in the light of Revelation's description of the fallen city of Babylon as "the habitation of devils, and the hold of every foul spirit, and a cage of every unclean and hateful bird" (18:2). Dostoevsky allows this motif to run further in the names he attributes to various of his characters, names that are derived from birds: thus Lebiadkin suggests *lebed'*, the word for "swan"; Drozdov comes from *drozd* (thrush); and Gaganov from *gaga* (eider). Moreover, Maria Lebiadkina expresses her disappointment in Stavrogin by referring to him as a "falcon" (*sokol*) who has turned into an owl (*filin*). Of course, there are many likely characters in *The Devils* whose names do not suggest birds, and it might well be argued that this weakens the above argument. It should be noted, though, that Dostoevsky makes more consistent use of names derived from birds in his previous novel *The Idiot*, a novel invested with the same darkly apocalyptic coloring.[20]

Geir Kjetsaa has drawn attention to further instances of apocalyptic symbolism in *The Devils*, as well as to annotations and markings in Dostoevsky's New Testament that appear to bear on the preoccupations of this novel. For example, alongside Revelation 17:11, referring to "the beast that was, and is not," Dostoevsky has written *obshchechelovek*, a concept closely related, as we have seen, to his critique of the Westernized intellectual and to his notebook conception of Stavrogin.[21] Further pursuit of such examples here is, however, redundant, for our main point is established: that Dostoevsky's intimate knowledge of St. John's Revelation allowed him in *The Devils* to transcend politics and to depict contemporary Russian sociopolitical reality as the fulfillment of apocalyptic prophecy. As Dostoevsky remarked in 1873 to Varvara Timofeeva, his coworker on the journal *The Citizen*, following a discussion of the penetration of European influences into Russia: "They don't suspect that soon it will be the end of everything, of all their 'progress' and idle chatter. They have no inkling that the Antichrist has already been born . . . and *he is coming!* . . . . The Antichrist is coming among us! And the end of the world is close – closer than people think!"[22]

The Great Sinner: (Mis)reading Stavrogin

From the moment in the working notebooks for *The Devils* when the Prince/Stavrogin figure emerged to prominence and displaced the earlier emphasis on politics, he acquired for Dostoevsky a clear centrality as the primary thematic and compositional principle in the novel. In an entry dated 10 April 1870, Dostoevsky noted: "And so, the novel's whole pathos lies with the Prince. He is the hero. All the rest moves around him, like a kaleidoscope" (11:136). In a later sketch, dated 16 August 1870, we read: "Everything is contained in the character of Stavrogin. Stavrogin is *everything*" (11:207). This centrality is built up gradually in the final novel, and Stavrogin's actual appearance is delayed until nearly one-third of the way through. Before that arrival his existence, as far as the reader is concerned, has consisted entirely of rumor and hearsay about his enigmatic behavior. He is surrounded by uncertainty, his personality is like a shadow cast by the expectations of others, and he comes in and out of focus like an optical illusion. When he does move from the fringes of rumor to the center of the novel's action, he retains this passive, intangible and ill-defined quality, haunting the novel and its characters like a ghost. Ralph Matlaw has described him memorably as "an empty, disappearing center."[23] We sense his immense gravitational pull at the heart of *The Devils*, but the nature of that pull is elusive; he hardly speaks or acts, we rarely penetrate his soul, and his being long remains an enigma to us. This was how Dostoevsky always intended it to be, for Stavrogin's role as the dark heart of the novel is structured on his great mystery. Whereas the lesser devils – Peter, Kirillov, Shigalev, and so on – skip about openly on the novel's stage, Stavrogin moves silently through its wings, only half seen but all-powerful in the influence he exercises over others. Like the beast of Revelation "that was, and is not," Stavrogin embodies mystery and evil. He is the life-denying principle, the spirit of negation and nonbeing, the vacuum left by a totally free will that has tired of its freedom and consumed itself.

The dramatic requirement that Stavrogin remain a half-grasped enigma must have been a major factor in Dostoevsky's decision not to restore the chapter "At Tikhon's" after that chapter was omitted from the initial serialization of the novel. The chapter, consisting of Stavrogin's revelation of his perverse past and his confession to the seduction of the young girl Matresha, was considered offensive by *The Russian Herald*. After several unsuccessful attempts to tone it down to requirements, Dostoevsky omitted it altogether, even from the later separate edition of the work. This failure to reinstate a chapter which he regarded initially as indispensible is partly explicable by Dostoevsky's unwillingness to undo consequent changes in the text occasioned by the original excision. But he may also have come to recognize that the value of Stavrogin's self-disclosure is undermined by its dramatic inconsistency: Stavrogin emerges best when the light is shone elsewhere, when his outline remains blurred but darkly suggestive. Most contemporary editions of *The Devils* offer "At Tikhon's" as an appendix, but some do restore the chapter to its original position, following chapter 8 of part 2.

The "meaning" of Stavrogin, what he is intended to represent, is revealed initially secondhand, as it were, through the analogies he evokes in the reader. Of course, different readers will identify different analogies, Stavrogin's very elusiveness allowing him to be all things to all men. The "political" reader, alert to the novel's origins in, and contribution to, the sociopolitical debates of its age, will seek his identity primarily in political terms, perhaps by offering real-life prototypes for the character. Thus several critics have suggested Nikolai Speshnev, Dostoevsky's "Mephistopheles" from his time in the Petrashevsky circle, as a probable model, and the Soviet scholar Grossman has argued that Stavrogin was intended to represent Bakunin, the éminence grise behind Nechaev and orchestrator of the Russian revolutionary movement.[24] The "literary" reader, on the other hand, alert above all else to the "fictionality" of Stavrogin, will recognize that he is a highly "artificial" character, ectoplasm summoned up from the European literary tradition and trailing clouds of literary allusion. The narrative devices Dostoevsky uses to create and sustain his air of mystery are, for example, those associated with the European gothic novel and the romantic tale of mystery. Robin Miller has examined Dostoevsky's debt to the English tale of terror, particularly the works of Ann Radcliffe, Horace Walpole, Matthew Lewis, and Charles Maturin, and has concluded aptly that "the language of the Gothic novel and its themes offered Dostoevsky a powerful rhetoric for describing modern man's predicament."[25] Stavrogin is, on the surface at least, a manifestation of this rhetoric. He is fashioned from the same devices of melodramatic excess as Maturin's *Melmoth the Wanderer,* and the scene describing his mother's impressions of him alone in his study incorporates the same atmosphere of overblown supernatural horror associated with the fictional depiction of vampires and vampirism:

Seeing that Nicholas was sitting somehow unnaturally still, she cautiously approached his divan with a beating heart. It was as though she were struck by how quickly he had fallen asleep and how he could sleep thus, sitting upright and so motionless; even his breathing was hardly noticeable. His face was pale and stern, but immobile as though it had completely frozen; his brows were slightly drawn together and frowning; he looked decidedly like a soulless wax figure. She stood over him for about three minutes, hardly drawing breath, and suddenly she was seized with terror. She withdrew on tiptoe, stopped in the doorway, hurriedly made the sign of the cross over him, and went away unobserved, her heart heavy with a new despair. (10:182)

This scene is a turning point in Varvara Petrovna's own "reading" of her son, as her traditional response to the presence of evil – the sign of the cross – implies. Hitherto, and in spite of her doubts, she has been prepared not to contradict openly the reassuring reading offered by Stepan Trofimovich, namely, that Stavrogin's perverse behavior is comparable to the youthful high spirits of Prince Hal in Shakespeare's *Henry IV,* "when he caroused with Falstaff, Poins, and Mistress Quickly" (10:36). Stavrogin's own reference to Captain Lebiadkin as his Falstaff (10:148) contributes to this misreading, but just as the untrustworthy Lebiadkin is no Falstaff, so too is the behavior of Stavrogin a far cry from Prince Harry's "turbulent outbursts of an overendowed nature." Instead, Stavrogin's nature turns out to be underendowed, corroded by its own spiritual and emotional bankruptcy and consumed by the tedium of an empty existence.

These qualities of Stavrogin offer the possibility of another literary reading: They suggest that he is a strangely anachronistic figure, a bored Byronic nobleman who has somehow strayed from the pages of Russian romantic fiction of the 1820s and 1830s into the political and social intrigues of a mid-nineteenth-century novel. His world-weariness, unpredictability, amoralism, and the ritual testing of his strength all call to mind such Byronic heroes as Eugene Onegin, from Pushkin's novel in verse of that name, and Pechorin in Lermontov's *A Hero of Our Time*. Byron and "Byronism" had been immensely popular in Russia in the early nineteenth century, and they had colored, in one way or another, the work of an entire generation of Russian writers. Dostoevsky saw Byronism, however, as an ultimately negative phenomenon in Russian life, describing Byron himself as a "bad little fellow." Imitation of his work and his literary heroes by Russians was part of that process of importing essentially foreign maladies not previously inherent in Russian culture and life (22:39–40). *The Diary of a Writer* for December 1877 offers an article on the poets Pushkin, Lermontov, and Nekrasov that brings into focus Dostoevsky's views on the significance of Byron and Byronism. He starts by insisting that the term *Byronist* should not be one of abuse, since "Byronism, though a momentary phenomenon, was a great, sacred, and necessary one in the life of European man, and perhaps in the life of the whole of humanity" (26:113). This was because Byron gave voice to "the dreadful anguish, disillusionment, and despair" that accompanied European cultural collapse following first the destruction of the ancien régime and then the implosion of the French Revolution. European man, deceived by the bankruptcy of revolutionary idealism, slumped into a destructive individualism to which Byron's heroes gave expression:

> The old idols lay shattered. And it was at this very moment that a great and mighty genius appeared, a passionate poet. In his melodies there resounded the anguish of mankind in those days and its gloomy disillusionment with its mission and with the ideals by which it had been deceived. This was a new and hitherto unheard-of muse of vengeance and sorrow, of cursing and despair. The spirit of Byronism suddenly seemed to possess the whole of humanity, everything responded to it. (26:114)

Not even Russia could avoid this response, if only out of compassion for what Europe was passing through. But, according to Dostoevsky, Pushkin – whose temperament and writings outgrew the effects of Byron – had demonstrated that Byronism was essentially alien to the Russian nature, the true reflection of which was to be found not among the Westernized elite but in the ordinary Russian people:

> The greatness of Pushkin, as a presiding genius, consisted precisely in the fact that, despite being surrounded by people who almost completely failed to understand him, he so soon discovered a firm path, a *great and longed-for way out for us Russians, and he pointed it out.* This way out was the people, *worship of the truth of the Russian people.* (26:114)

These are arguments familiar to us through our earlier analysis of Dostoevsky's views on nationality. Stavrogin's Byronism marks him as emblematic of the Russian nobleman's alienation from his roots; the emptiness of his existence depicts the results of such alienation. As Joseph Frank has reminded us, Dostoevsky acknowledged that the questioning of national identity that gave rise to both the Westernizer and the Slavophile movements was itself a product of this alienation, and it is therefore apt that in *The Devils* the rootless and Byronic Stavrogin should be revealed as the source of ideological inspiration for both the Westernizer Kirillov and the Slavophile Shatov.[26]

The semantic weight thus attached to Byron and Byronism perhaps helps to explain an otherwise odd aspect of *The Devils:* its persistent fascination with lameness. The most obvious manifestation of this is Stavrogin's legal wife Maria Lebiadkina, who is crippled; but the motif of lameness and broken legs also reappears several times in relation to Stavrogin's mistress, Liza Tushina. When Peter Verkhovensky recounts how he nearly broke a leg when his train was derailed, Liza reacts hysterically: "Mama, dear Mama, don't be afraid if I really do break both legs. It could easily happen; you yourself are often saying that I ride every day at breakneck speed. Mavrikii Nikolaevich, will you lead me about when I'm lame?" (10:157). Later, the infatuated Lebiadkin composes a poetic declaration of love for Liza, entitled "If She Should Break a Leg."

Such references are primarily intended to forge a link between Liza and Maria Lebiadkina, and they also contribute to the novel's demonic texture since lameness was a characteristic attributed to the devil in Russian folklore; but the motif of lameness also had strong Byronic associations for Dostoevsky. In his working drafts for *The Diary of a Writer* for February 1876 he observed: "I am convinced (well, at least a little) that had Byron not been lame, then perhaps he would not have written his *Cain* or *Childe Harold*, or rather he would have written them differently" (22:184). This same observation is repeated on no fewer than five other occasions in Dostoevsky's notes.[27] The same association of Byron with lameness/leg-breaking is also to be found, albeit in grotesque form, in the story "Uncle's Dream" (1859) when the uncle recalls meeting Byron abroad:

I remember Lord Byron. We were on friendly terms. He danced the Cracovienne divinely at the Vienna Congress. . . . However, perhaps that wasn't Lord Byron, but somebody else. To be sure, it wasn't Lord Byron, but a certain Pole! I remember it all now. And an extremely original chap that Pole was, too! He made himself out to be a count, but it transpired that he ran some sort of cookhouse. But he danced the Cracovienne divinely, and ended up by breaking his leg. I wrote a verse about the incident there and then:

> Our Pole
> Loved the Polish dance . . .
> But he broke his leg,
> And thereafter missed his chance. (2:313–14)

There is a cluster of serious points behind this nonsense: The mention of a Byronic pretender and the composition of a poem about a broken leg tie "Uncle's Dream" to *The Devils*. As the editors of the Academy edition indicate, in creating the figure of the uncle, who forever pretends to be what he is not, Dostoevsky drew on a literary model of the impostor: Khlestakov from Gogol's comedy *The Government Inspector* (2:517). The theme of imposture also, of course, attaches to Stavrogin, most openly in the scene where Maria Lebiadkina sees through him with the words: "Grishka Otrepev – anathema!" – a reference to the false claimant to the Russian throne during the succession crisis of 1598–1613. The notebooks for *The Devils* cite Khlestakov directly, but in connection with the arrival of Peter Verkhovensky; in the novel itself it is left to the narrator to suggest indirectly the link between that literary watchword for imposture and Stavrogin. He dutifully reports rumors that Stavrogin is secretly a government official, that he has arrived incognito on a confidential mission, and that he reports back to Petersburg (10:168). The narrator is unconscious of the literary identity he thus unwittingly assigns to Stavrogin, but Dostoevsky's "literary" reader would see through these details to the plot and the central figure of Gogol's *The Government Inspector.*

Of all the literary allusions trailed by Stavrogin, the most obvious, and perhaps the most significant, is to Pechorin, the disillusioned Byronic protagonist of Lermontov's *A Hero of Our Time.* Indeed, at one point in the novel the narrator reports Liputin's scornful dismissal of Stavrogin as a "Pechorin-ladykiller" (10:84). We should note in passing just how unauthoritative this analogy is: It does not come directly from the author but takes the form of another character's subjective opinion refracted through the voice of a narrator whose own insight and trustworthiness are limited. This is important to our argument, which is that Stavrogin is essentially a noncharacter, an ever-shifting and indefinite composite, whose meaning is derived from the readings and misreadings of both the other characters in the novel and the reader himself. The allusions to Pechorin continue with Stavrogin's arrival in the novel, when the narrator offers a sustained comparison of the newcomer with Lermontov himself, concluding that Stavrogin has far outstripped the latter's malice and ennui (10:165). When Peter Verkhovensky visits Stavrogin in his room to suggest the elimination of the Lebiadkins, he notices that Stavrogin has been reading an expensive volume of illustrations of *The Women of Balzac* (10:180). The significance of this passes Peter by, but the reader familiar with *A Hero of Our Time* will recall that in that work Pechorin himself is likened to a "thirty-year-old Balzacian coquette after a particularly exhausting dance."[28]

There are many other points of contact between Stavrogin and Pechorin,[29] but these only serve to draw our attention to the spiritual affinity of the two characters. In his lukewarm malice, his stuttering gestures of will, his aching emptiness, his indifference and loss of all conviction, Stavrogin suggests the horrifying end of romantic revolt. His tragedy is that of the man who has sacrificed his own personality on the altar of personal freedom. In his pursuit of totally unfettered self-will he has liberated himself from all spiritual, emotional, and intellectual bonds, only to find the "freedom" thus attained to be a sterile conceit. A man without convictions, without warmth, without enthusiasm no longer has a use for freedom, for there is no longer meaning in his life. At the end of *A Hero of Our Time* Pechorin has acknowledged that his freedom is a burden, and he sets off on his travels in an attempt to fill the emptiness of his existence. At the end of *Notes from Underground* the hero's perverse drive for complete freedom has diluted his being to the point where he cannot even construct a coherent sentence: After all, how can one express oneself when there is no longer a self to express? Stavrogin has surpassed them both: In him total freedom becomes total nonbeing. He has no belief in himself, or in anything outside himself, on which to base his existence. He is empty and inactive, a black hole at the center of the novel. His wearisome freedom condemns him to such inertia that he is incapable of anything. Even in the murder of the Lebiadkins, Stavrogin's role is entirely passive: Peter Verkhovensky is his will and Fedka is his proxy. Stavrogin remains a collapsed character, a dead sun, emitting neither light nor heat but nevertheless trapping all the other characters in his gravitational field. He is persuaded of the truth of Shatov's warning that unless he finds some purpose to his life, he will "disappear like rotten mildew" (10:203), and, as Richard Peace has observed, the chapters entitled "Night" mark his attempts to discover existential certainty among the ruins of his past.[30] He revisits Shatov and Kirillov, who now espouse ideologies Stavrogin once inspired but has long since discarded, but he is bored by them, just as he is bored by Peter and his political dreams, by his love affair with Liza, and by the attempts of Dasha Shatova to save his empty soul. Even his suicide is the result of apathy rather than conviction: The shabby practicality of its preparations – a greased rope nailed to a door – lacks all rhetorical flourish. It is a bare confirmation of what we have known all along – that Stavrogin is devoid of life.

As Dostoevsky signaled in his notebooks, everything moves around Stavrogin like a kaleidoscope, and he is the focus of every other character's designs. All are drawn to him, only to meet disappointment or destruction. As the novel progresses the void of his personality is filled, not by his own spiritual growth but by the misreading of him by others. "I invented you when we were abroad. I invented you when I looked at you. If I hadn't looked at you from out of my corner, none of it would have entered my head!" says Peter Verkhovensky (10:326), who finds in Stavrogin the legendary figurehead through which his own political ambitions will be realized. "You're just what we need. I . . . I particularly need someone like you. I know of nobody quite like you. You are my leader, my sun, and I am your worm!" (10:324). Other characters, too, invent their own Stavrogin. Kirillov looks at him and sees confirmation of his ideas on the metamorphosis of man through will: "Remember what you've meant in my life, Stavrogin!" (10:189). He is central to Shatov's Russian messianism: "I can't tear you out of my heart, Nikolai Stavrogin!" (10:202). He is the focus of Liza Tushina's unhealthy preoccupation with evil, her demon of darkness. The well-meaning Dasha Shatova fixes on his potential for self-renewal. And the imagination of the unfortunate Maria Lebiadkina, steeped in popular religious symbolism, mistakes the emotional emptiness of the nationally disengaged *obshchechelovek* for the nobility of a savior-prince drawn from a rich native folk tradition.

Inevitably, Stavrogin disappoints them all in the end. He spurns Kirillov and Shatov, leaving them to empty ideologies, for no idea bequeathed by Stavrogin can be fertile. The convictions of both, although fanatically held by them, are corrupted by their origins in Stavrogin. Like their source, these ideas are shells surrounding an empty center: Shatov's religio-nationalist fervor fails to disguise a basic lack of faith, and Kirillov's militant atheism and intoxication with man's freedom are negated, first, by his paradoxical love of God and God's creation and, second, by his own intellectual servitude. He fails to see that in feeling *compelled* to proclaim his freedom through suicide, he has relinquished that very freedom. Stavrogin also fails to live up to the expectations of his women: He is no more capable of serving Liza's fascination with evil than he is of satisfying Dasha's hopes of salvation, for he is beyond all moral definition.

In his disappointment Peter Verkhovensky, like Maria Lebiadkina earlier, lays at Stavrogin's door the charge of imposture. Stavrogin's inability to be the America to Peter's Columbus elicits the furious retort that he is a lying, worthless little aristocrat (10:326). These particular accusations of imposture, however, represent yet another misreading of Stavrogin: He is no Khlestakov. Imposture implies a conscious act of deception, whereas Stavrogin's followers are largely guilty of self-deception in the identities they have ascribed to their "idol." It is significant that Peter Verkhovensky's accusation comes at the point in the novel where it does, at the very end of part 2, chapter 8, for this chapter was originally to have been followed by the omitted chapter "At Tikhon's," a chapter in which Stavrogin does assume the mantle of impostor. "At Tikhon's" consists of a written document in which Stavrogin confesses to the violation of a twelve-year-old girl, framed by a discussion with the monk Tikhon in which he announces his intention to purge his guilt by publishing his confession. The significance of this document lies in the fact that it is the only place in the novel where Stavrogin attempts a sustained "reading" of himself; this alone is enough to explain Dostoevsky's initial despair at its exclusion.

The chapter prepares the ground for Stavrogin's attempt at self-revelation by referring initially to the misreading of him by others: Tikhon reveals his familiarity with the rumors that abound in the town. He himself then contributes to this process of misreading when he insists that he met Stavrogin in the monastery four years earlier. Stavrogin denies this with the words: "You have perhaps only heard about me and have formed some sort of impression, and that's why you're confused about having seen me" (11:7). But these early exchanges also implicitly warn of the nature of the confession that is to follow and how we should approach it: "It was as though [Stavrogin] had decided on something extraordinary and incontestable, *but at the same time almost impossible for him*" (11:7, my emphasis). Moreover, he admits to suffering from hallucinations in which he sees the devil, concluding: "Of course I see him. I see him like I am seeing you. . . . But sometimes I see him and I am not convinced that I am seeing him, even though I can see him. . . . And sometimes I'm not sure what I am seeing, *and I don't know what is real: him or me*" (11:9, my emphasis). We must ask ourselves how capable of self-confession such a man is, when he is so clearly incapable of both self-recognition and self-expression.

And so it proves: Stavrogin's confession, for all its shocking detail, turns out to be as opaque and elusive as the man himself. It is, in fact, a travesty of a confession, an exercise in self-evasion, rather than self-revelation. Its motivation is also inverted: It is driven not by contrition but by scorn for those who might condemn him. It is crafted not out of the desire for confessional openness, but, like the revelations of the Underground Man, from an implicitly dialogical sensitivity to what others might think. It is mannered, rhetorical, and as devoid of real content as Stavrogin himself. Tikhon recognizes that Stavrogin "presents himself" (11:24) with one eye on his audience, and his suggestion that Stavrogin might work on the style of the document suggests a sarcasm unexpected in one of his calling.

Stavrogin's only other attempt at a reading of himself is found in his final letter to Dasha. This is not as sustained as his confession, but, on the other hand, it lacks the latter's pretense. In it he finally confronts his withered spirit, his rootlessness, and the emptiness of his life:

I am not attached to anything in Russia – everything here is as alien to me as everywhere else. . . . I've tested my powers everywhere. . . . But what to apply those powers to, that's what I never could see and can't see even now. . . . My desires are too weak; they cannot be a guide to me. You can cross a river on a log, but not on a chip of wood. . . . Only negation has flowed from me, without magnanimity and without force. Not even negation. Everything is always so petty and stale. (10:513–14)

At last we are reading the "real" Stavrogin: The style of the letter is as arid as the desert of his soul and, in case we miss the point, Dostoevsky has his narrator draw attention to its shortcomings: "Here is the letter, word for word, without correcting the smallest mistake in the style of this Russian son of the nobility, who never quite mastered Russian grammar for all his European education" (10:513). This sly comment on the letter's literary qualities returns us to the idea in Dostoevsky's notebooks from which everything has sprung: that of the great sinner, the *obshchechelovek* torn from his native soil, from his people and his God, and condemned thereafter to limbo.

Conclusion: The Reception of *The Devils*

The Devils was serialized in *The Russian Herald* between January 1871 and December 1872, and it subsequently appeared as a separate book edition in 1873. There was a lengthy gap in its periodical publication between November 1871 and November 1872 that was initially owing to Katkov's unwillingness to publish "At Tikhon's" and Dostoevsky's desperate efforts to salvage the chapter. This initial hiatus in the novel's serialization was extended by Katkov's subsequent decision to wait for the work's completion before resuming publication. As we have seen, Dostoevsky eventually decided against the restoration of the excised chapter, even for the separate edition. It was discovered among his papers after the Bolshevik Revolution and first published in 1922. Dostoevsky's working notebooks for *The Devils* appeared in print for the first time in 1935.[31] The critical reception of *The Devils* in Russia was dominated by the hostility of the liberal and progressive press. The general view was that this was a work driven by indignation rather than inspiration and that in it Dostoevsky had vilified the progressive intelligentsia by his concentration on atypical individuals. *The St. Petersburg News* in 1873 dismissed the work as "a phantasmagoria created by a sick imagination" (no. 6, 6 January 1873), while in the same year two revolutionary populist critics, N. K. Mikhailovsky and P. N. Tkachev offered the most sustained condemnations of the novel as a libel on revolutionary youth.[32] *The Devils*, along with the rest of Dostoevsky's work, received a more favorable reappraisal at the turn of the century, by which time a major change had taken place in the Russian intelligentsia. In the period of political reaction following the assassination of Tsar Alexander II in 1881, shortly after Dostoevsky's death, intellectuals sought refuge from social and political reality through the cultivation of mysticism and aestheticism. For such readers *The Devils* offered richer pickings, and their attention was drawn away from the novel's political complexion and toward the spiritual and philosophical problems Stavrogin posed. The politics of *The Devils* reemerged as a major obstacle in its critical appraisal during the Soviet period, and it long remained unpublished except in collected academic editions of Dostoevsky's works. E. N. Konshina's edition of the notebooks for *The Devils* was prefaced by a brave attempt to justify such interest in an ideologically suspect novel during the Stalinist period. Russian critical interest in the novel has revived in the post-Soviet period as commentators have rediscovered its "prophetic" qualities.[33]

The Devils was the last of Dostoevsky's great novels to be translated into English. Constance Garnett's admirable version appeared in 1914, under the title *The Possessed*, and elicited considerable critical interest at a time when Dostoevsky's reputation in the English-speaking world was expanding toward the full-blown "Dostoevsky cult" that followed John Middleton Murry's excessive and enthusiastic study of 1916.[34] The London periodical *The Athenæum* commented on the novel's "637 pages of anything but diluted matter" and its "extraordinary handling of psychological abnormality"[35] with an enthusiasm that suggested that its preoccupation with the grotesque and abnormal – qualities that had alienated its earliest Russian critics – had at last found an enthusiastic readership in a world where the certainties of the Edwardian era were about to be destroyed in the nightmare of the First World War. Garnett's translation, accurate but quaint and linguistically dated in places, has been superseded by more modern versions, the most recent of which are those by Michael R. Katz (1992) and Richard Pevear and Larissa Volokhonsky (1994).[36]

It is impossible in an introduction of this length to do justice to Dostoevsky's critical reception in the West or to disentangle critical responses to *The Devils* from that general reception. Fortunately, the job of documenting how Dostoevsky's reputation was established outside Russia has been well done elsewhere.[37] It is probably fair to say that that reputation has been erected primarily on *The Brothers Karamazov, Crime and Punishment,* and, to a lesser extent, *The Idiot.* These, rather than *The Devils,* have proved to be the most accessible of Dostoevsky's novels for his foreign readers, and they have attracted most critical attention, both academic and nonacademic. For example, Hermann Hesse's *In Sight of Chaos* (1923) focuses on Dostoevsky's sense of European cultural collapse, but its gaze is directed primarily at *The Brothers Karamazov* and *The Idiot.* André Gide's *Dostoievsky* (1923) and Thomas Mann's *Dostoevsky – In Moderation* (1948) examine Dostoevsky's preoccupation with complex psychology and the morbid and pathological, but they give no special emphasis to *The Devils.* Sigmund Freud's famous essay *Dostoevsky and Parricide* concentrates on *The Brothers Karamazov,* even though the theme of father-son relations is central also to *The Devils.* The exception to this general rule is Albert Camus, who manifested a particular interest in *The Devils.* His *Le mythe de Sisyphe* (1942) draws particularly on the "logical suicide" of Kirillov in order to stake its claim that Dostoevsky was an existentialist, while *L'Homme révolté* (1951) discusses Shigalev as a prophet of twentieth-century totalitarianism.

It is not difficult to see how these priorities were established: Superficially at least, *The Devils* is more deeply embedded than the other novels in the world of mid-nineteenth-century Russian ideological clashes, a world that recedes ever further with each passing year. Yet, it has been the purpose of this introduction to demonstrate that the true impact of that work lies not primarily in its polemical intent nor in its vivid, if jaundiced account of the Russian revolutionary movement. It lies instead in the way *The Devils* incarnates those qualities of narrative sophistication, psychological insight, and philosophical depth that confer greatness on all Dostoevsky's mature work.

NOTES

1. Translated by the author from F. M. Dostoevskii, *Polnoe sobranie sochinenii v 30-i tomakh* (Leningrad: Nauka, 1972–90) (hereafter referred to as *PSS*), vol. 27:65. All future references to Dostoevsky's works are to this edition and are given in the text (e.g., 27:65).

2. For detailed analysis of this aspect of Dostoevsky's narrative, see M. M. Bakhtin, *Problems of Dostoevsky's Poetics*, translated by Caryl Emerson (Manchester: Manchester University Press, 1984); and S. B. Vladiv, *Narrative Principles in Dostoevskij's "Besy": A Structural Analysis* (Berne: Peter Lang, 1979).

3. Joseph Frank, *Dostoevsky: The Stir of Liberation, 1860–1865* (Princeton, N.J.: Princeton University Press, 1986), 233.

4. For a detailed analysis of Slavophile ideology, see A. Walicki, *The Slavophile Controversy* (Oxford: Oxford University Press, 1975).

5. See *PSS*, 12:161–253.

6. Fyodor Dostoevsky, *The Notebooks for "The Possessed"*, edited by Edward Wasiolek, translated by Victor Terras (Chicago: University of Chicago Press, 1968).

7. See *PSS*, 12:163, passim.

8. Bakhtin, *Problems of Dostoevsky's Poetics*, chap. 4.

9. See, for example, Franco Venturi, *Roots of Revolution: A History of the Populist and Socialist Movements in Nineteenth-Century Russia*, translated by F. Haskell (London: Weidenfeld and Nicolson, 1960), chap. 15.

10. Geir Kjetsaa, *Fyodor Dostoevsky: A Writer's Life*, translated by Siri Hustvedt and David McDuff (London: Macmillan, 1987), 251.

11. Dostoevsky, *The Notebooks for "The Possessed,"* 5–6.

12. Joseph Frank, *Dostoevsky: The Miraculous Years, 1865–1871* (Princeton, N.J.: Princeton University Press, 1995), 425–29.

13. R. L. Jackson, *The Art of Dostoevsky: Deliriums and Nocturnes* (Princeton, N.J.: Princeton University Press, 1981), 210–11.

14. Ibid., 210.

15. See *PSS*, 12:203–11.

16. See Frank, *Dostoevsky: The Miraculous Years*, 450; and *PSS*, 12:211.

17. This view is advanced by the editors in *PSS*, 12:223.

18. See W. J. Leatherbarrow, *Fedor Dostoevsky* (Boston: G. K. Hall, 1981), 127–29; and Kjetsaa, *Fyodor Dostoevsky*, 253–61.

19. See W. J. Leatherbarrow, ed., *Dostoevskii and Britain* (Oxford: Berg, 1995), 6–10.

20. Leatherbarrow, *Fedor Dostoevsky*, 98–103.

21. Geir Kjetsaa, *Dostoevsky and His New Testament* (Oslo: Humanities Press, 1984), 77.

22. F. M. *Dostoevskii v vospominaniiakh sovremennikov*, edited by A. Dolinin (Moscow: GIKhL, 1964), 2:170.

23. Ralph Matlaw, *The Brothers Karamazov: Novelistic Technique* (The Hague: Mouton, 1957), 37.

24. For arguments for and against this proposition, see L. P. Grossman and V. P. Polonskii, *Spor o Bakunine i Dostoevskom* (Leningrad: GIZ, 1926).

25. In Leatherbarrow, *Dostoevskii and Britain*, 140.

26. Frank, *Dostoevsky: The Miraculous Years*, 467–71. Frank also addresses the historico-chronological problem posed by the fact that the novel presents Stepan Trofimovich, a liberal Westernizer of the 1840s, as the spiritual teacher of Stavrogin, who represents the Byronic nobleman of the previous generation.

27. See *PSS*, 22:246; and 24:75, 82, 102, 133.

28. M. Iu. Lermontov, *Polnoe sobranie sochinenii* (Moscow: Academia, 1937), 5:224.

29. See E. Stenbock-Fermor, "Lermontov and Dostoevskij's Novel *The Devils*," *Slavonic and East European Journal* 17 (1959): 215–30.

30. Richard Peace, *Dostoyevsky: An Examination of the Major Novels* (Cambridge: Cambridge University Press, 1971), 185.

31. E. N. Konshina, *Zapisnye tetradi F. M. Dostoevskogo* (Moscow: Academia, 1935).

32. N. K. Mikhailovskii, *Sochineniia* (St. Petersburg: Russkoe bogatstvo,

1896), 1:840–72; and P. N. Tkachev, *Izbrannye sochineniia na sotsial'no-politicheskie temy* (Moscow: Sotsekgiz, 1932–37), 3:5–48.

33. L. Saraskina, *Besy: Roman-preduprezhdenie* (Moscow: Sovetskii pisatel', 1990).

34. J. Middleton Murry, *Fyodor Dostoevsky: A Critical Study* (London: Martin Secker, 1916).

35. *The Athenæum*, no. 4499, 17 January 1914, 89.

36. Fyodor Dostoevsky, *Devils*, translated by Michael R. Katz (Oxford: Oxford University Press, 1992); Fyodor Dostoevsky, *Demons*, translated by Richard Pevear and Larissa Volokhonsky (New York: Knopf, 1994).

37. For an account of Dostoevsky's reception in the English-speaking world, see Helen Muchnic, *Dostoevsky's English Reputation, 1881–1936* (New York: Octagon, 1969).

II CRITICISM

The Devils in the Context
of Contemporary Russian
Thought and Politics

D. C. OFFORD

Russian critics of Dostoevsky's time, particularly those of radical persuasion, tended to look on imaginative literature as a mirror held up to an easily definable concrete reality. They expected writers to attempt a more or less objective description of contemporary types and problems and accused them of distortion of reality if its reflection in a given work of art did not conform to their own perception of it. Thus the prominent critic, revolutionary activist, and leading exponent of "Jacobinism,"[1] P. N. Tkachev, took Dostoevsky to task in a celebrated review of *The Devils* for presenting in his nihilists not the "characters of living people" drawn from the reality he imagined he was studying but "mannequins."[2]

The modern literary scholar or intellectual historian, on the other hand, is likely to approach even the prose fiction of the Russian age of realism as a prism through which reality is refracted rather than a mirror that distinctly reflects it. With regard to *The Devils*, in particular, we should want to register at the outset several reservations about the nature and accuracy of its depiction of contemporary "reality." First, as a work of art the novel is bound to have its own dynamic and exigencies that outweigh any requirement for the objectivity of historiography. Second, its account of events comes to us through a narrator who at times assumes authorial omniscience but who is also presented as partial, not fully informed, and limited in understanding. Third, such is the multiplicity of perspectives in a Dostoevskian novel that much of our evidence for anything – facts, events, character – takes the form of highly tendentious or, for some other reason, unreliable accounts given by characters themselves. The main exegesis of Shigalev's "system," for example, emanates not from Shigalev but from the lame teacher and Peter Verkhovensky. Fourth, Dostoevsky is not fair-minded, except in the higher sense that as an artist he baulks at things that seem to him to lack aesthetic or spiritual truthfulness.

Nevertheless, there does exist a close, though complex relationship between *The Devils* and the social, political, intellectual, and cultural environment from which it springs. On one level, Dostoevsky has used what are described in the introduction to this volume as "current political realia." There is a wealth of allusion to the events and the social and political turmoil of the time. Moreover, the activity and personalities of certain notable, or notorious, contemporaries of Dostoevsky lie behind some of his portraits. Without an awareness of at least some of this allusion, the modern reader may find the novel relatively inaccessible. At a deeper level, the novel engages with schools of Russian thought, with which the Russian literary tradition is in any case closely interrelated, in order to produce a distinctive statement of its own on the condition of Russia. This statement has both its negative and positive aspects. The negative aspect, which is overwhelmingly prevalent in the novel, represents a sustained critique of liberal and socialist values, which Dostoevsky tends – perversely, a Western reader is likely to feel – to see as inextricably interlinked and essentially similar. The positive aspect, which is more implicit than explicit, belongs to the romantic conservative stream of Russian thought and has its antecedents in the Slavophilism of the 1840s and the more recent *pochvennichestvo*, or "native soil conservatism," which Dostoevsky himself had helped to formulate in the early 1860s following his return from the purgatory of Siberian exile.[3] In its function as an independent contribution to the vigorous intellectual, cultural, and spiritual life of the intelligentsia, *The Devils* itself becomes a factor in, and exerts its own influence on, contemporary reality.

My task in this chapter, therefore, is threefold: first, in section 1, to examine the novel's location at that point in the turbulent reality of post-reform Russia at which the revolutionary movement, which was eventually to topple the ancien régime, began to develop; second, in sections 2–4, to follow Dostoevsky's analysis of the moral and spiritual failings within the educated class which he believes have brought the country to this critical condition (in the process, I examine in succession the so-called "liberal" and "nihilist" camps and the dissociation from their native culture which Dostoevsky believed was common to both); third, in section 5, to look for the rays that give hope in the darkness of the novel and identify the landmarks that Russians will need, in Dostoevsky's opinion, to keep in sight if they are not altogether to lose their moral bearings.

1. Revolutionary Russia

In the first half of the 1860s the Russian autocracy, persuaded by Russia's defeat in the Crimean War (1853–56) of the necessity of far-reaching change, had abolished the age-old institution of serfdom and introduced additional consequential reforms, approved by the tsar in 1864, in the legal system and the system of local government. There is a wealth of contemporary reference in *The Devils* that locates the novel in the fluid reality of post-reform Russia. The narrator refers to the emancipation edict of 1861 and the difficulties some of the nobility had in coming to terms with it (10:224). Characters debate the merits of the new law courts (10:233–34). There is mention of the *zemstva*, organs of limited local self-government that began to be established in 1865 (10:247), as well as such other regular features of nineteenth-century Russian life as outbreaks of cholera and cattle disease (e.g., 10:484).

At the same time the young radical wing of the intelligentsia, which in the years immediately following the Crimean War had begun comprehensively to define its differences from the older more moderate Westernizers, became increasingly militant. At first, under the influence of N. G. Chernyshevsky and N. A. Dobroliubov, this wing of the intelligentsia had challenged the conceptions of the older generation on such subjects as the nature of beauty and the function of art, human nature, moral goodness, and the desirable extent and permissible means of social and political change. By the middle of the 1860s, under the influence of D. I. Pisarev and spurred on by a sense of frustration at what was perceived in radical quarters as the limited extent of the "great reforms," this challenge to the older values had turned into an impatient, intolerant, destructive "nihilism." This frustration had begun to find expression in 1861–62 in student disorders and in the emergence of revolutionary groups and then, in the mid-1860s, in the formation of further conspiratorial groups in Moscow and St. Petersburg led by N. A. Ishutin and I. A. Khudiakov, respectively. On 4 April 1866 a student named D. V. Karakozov, who belonged to the melodramatically styled group "Hell," an offshoot of Ishutin's organization, carried out an unsuccessful attempt on the life of Alexander II. A further expression of the growing unrest was the appearance in 1861–62 of various types of agitational literature – proclamations, leaflets, appeals – printed by conspiratorial groups either in emigration or on clandestine printing presses inside Russia. Society was also alarmed by a series of fires that broke out in St. Petersburg in May 1862, responsibility for which was attributed by conservative circles to the "nihilists." The early stages of this intellectual and political turmoil are observed in the opening chapter of *The Devils*, when the narrator acidly describes the circles in which Stepan Verkhovensky and Varvara Stavrogina move during their stay in St. Petersburg in the early 1860s. An unruly crowd of literati feverishly debates such matters as the peasant reform, the recent proclamations, women's rights, and the abolition of the army, navy, clergy, the family, and – Dostoevsky cannot resist a touch of absurdity – even children (10:22).

By the end of the 1860s the government, alarmed by the growing militancy of the intelligentsia, the signs of unrest in Russia, and the Polish Revolt of 1863, had lost its reforming ardor. And yet the revolutionary tide continued to swell. It derived impetus from the vigorous socialist movement in Western Europe, where an International Working Men's Association (that is, the First International) had been established in 1864. Athough it was to founder in 1872 on the hostility between Karl Marx, who envisaged a period of "dictatorship of the proletariat," and M. A. Bakunin, who as an anarchist wished to see the state destroyed in all its forms, the International enjoyed the reputation of a formidable force with huge membership and resources. Socialists were also inspired by the Paris Commune of March–May 1871, a republican insurrection against the provisional national government of France. The vitality of international socialism at this period is keenly felt in *The Devils*. There are repeated hints at, or rumors of, the international connections of the secret society being created in the novel by Peter Verkhovensky (e.g., 10:193). Reference is made to a recent congress of the League of Peace and Freedom in Geneva (10:77) at one of whose sessions Dostoevsky himself had heard fiery oratory about revolutionary destruction.[4] (Even the arch-destroyer Bakunin, though, is outdone by Dostoevsky's Kirillov, who apparently requires more than a million heads for the establishment of good sense in Europe [10:77], and by Liamshin, who would blow up nine-tenths of the population [10:312–13].) Nor is it coincidental that members of the younger generation (Kirillov, Shatov, Maria Shatova, Stavrogin, Liza Tushina, Peter Verkhovensky) have gravitated in the years before the time at which the main part of *The Devils* is set toward Switzerland and, in particular, Geneva. For Switzerland, with its relative political freedom, had become a haven for leading socialist émigrés, including Bakunin himself.

Reverberations of the international socialist movement were felt in Russia in the growing unrest of the late 1860s among the idealistic and discontented student population and, in particular, in disorders in the higher educational institutions of St. Petersburg and Moscow in the academic year 1868–69. This unrest was harnessed by S. G. Nechaev, a cunning, beguiling young *meshchanin*[5] from the provincial textile-manufacturing town of Ivanovo, who succeeded in organizing a number of circles in St. Petersburg before disappearing in March 1869 and fleeing to Geneva, where he won the confidence of the gullible Bakunin and of N. P. Ogarev, A. I. Herzen's lifelong friend now enfeebled by infirmity and alcohol. Together with these émigrés Nechaev generated a further torrent of proclamations, written in a vengeful spirit and millenarian tone, hundreds of copies of which were posted to Russia from abroad during the spring and summer of 1869.[6] Returning to Russia in August 1869, armed with a melodramatic document signed by Bakunin bearing the seal of a "European Revolutionary Alliance," Nechaev again set about organizing student circles in Moscow under the banner of a "Committee of the People's Revenge."

The notoriety which Nechaev quickly earned arose in general from his espousal of the principle that the attainment of the end of revolution in Russia was of such overriding importance that the use of any means, including deception, extortion, blackmail, theft, and even murder, was legitimate in its pursuit. From the pages of the infamous "Catechism of a Revolutionary," which Nechaev probably wrote in collaboration with Bakunin in the summer of 1869 and which was read out at the trial of his coconspirators in July 1871, there emerged a picture of the revolutionary as a ruthless, self-abnegating figure whose personal wants and feelings have been wholly subordinated to the exigencies of the revolutionary struggle.[7] Above all, Nechaev's notoriety stemmed from his orchestration and execution of the murder, on 21 November 1869 in a grotto in a remote part of the grounds of the Agricultural Academy in Moscow, of I. I. Ivanov, a student who was evidently less pliable than the other members of Nechaev's cell and whom Nechaev suspected of intending to betray the organization. Ivanov was lured to the grotto by a request for help to recover printing equipment that was supposed to have been buried there by Ishutin and was set on and pinned down by members of the group while Nechaev beat and strangled him and finally shot him in the head. His body, weighted with bricks, was thrown through a hole that Nechaev had made in the ice on the pond next to the grotto. Nechaev's hands were badly bitten during the struggle and his hat was carelessly left at the scene of the crime. It is possible that what Nechaev claimed was an accident with his gun when the murderers were cleaning themselves in the rooms of one of their number after the murder was, in fact, an attempt by Nechaev to kill one of his accomplices, I. G. Pryzhov, with a view to blaming the murder on him. Nechaev left Moscow for St. Petersburg the following day. Ivanov's body was discovered on 25 November, and arrests and confessions followed shortly. Nechaev himself again fled the country in the middle of December 1869. The members of his network, who came to be known as *Nechaevtsy*, were brought to trial in 1871. Nechaev was betrayed by a member of the Russian émigré colony in Switzerland in August 1872, arrested in Zurich, and extradited to Russia. He was tried in January 1873 and incarcerated in the Peter and Paul Fortress in St. Petersburg, from which he had claimed in 1869 to have made an audacious escape. There he died on 21 November 1882.

The similarities between Nechaev's activities and those of Peter Verkhovensky in *The Devils* are numerous and striking. Like Nechaev, Peter Verkhovensky is creating a secret society supposedly consisting of a central committee with international connections and a pan-Russian network of innumerable small cells that operate in isolation from one another, in secrecy, and in strict subordination to the center. The broad aim of the organization, as defined by Shigalev and as described in its program, which is quoted word for word by Liamshin in his confession to the police, is systematically to undermine, confuse, and demoralize society, and then, when society is shaken, sick, cynical, and without faith, to seize control of it (10:418, 510). Peter's arrangement and execution of Shatov's murder is famously reminiscent of Nechaev's murder of Ivanov. It takes place outside a grotto at a remote forested spot by some ponds on the edge of the Stavrogin park and Peter involves as many of the other members of his cell in the murder as possible (part 3, chap. 6, 1). His willing assistant in this enterprise is the young ensign Erkel who, as one fanatically devoted to the "common cause" and prepared to carry out any of Peter's instructions (10:439), is based, to some extent, on Nechaev's unquestioning disciple N. N. Nikolaev. Like Nikolaev, Erkel on his master's instructions, plays the role at meetings of a silent observer or "inspector" (10:304, 415), goes to fetch the victim on the night of the murder (10:454), and, at the moment of the killing, helps to restrain him.⁸ The failure of the flustered murderers to remove Shatov's hat from the scene of the crime, the savage bite that Kirillov inflicts on Peter's finger, and Peter's attempt to use Kirillov's shooting of himself as a means of diverting suspicion from the real culprit all vaguely suggest details of the story of Ivanov's murder and its aftermath.

In method, too, Peter Verkhovensky resembles the Nechaevan conspirator who emerges from the pages of the "Catechism of a Revolutionary." He is a skilled "political seducer" (10:512) who, through a combination of flattery, speciousness, and feigned mediocrity, achieves acceptance and considerable influence in local society. At the same time he soon becomes noted in the town for eavesdropping, reporting on people, and having the members of his organization spy on one another (10:417–18, 298). He attempts to compromise people (he borrows and for a long time will not return von Lembke's manuscript of his novel which the governor has foolishly lent him [10:245]). He incriminates allies: The murder of Lebiadkin and his sister has been conceived by Peter as a means of securing Stavrogin's dependency on him (10:511). He is a liar who spreads stories that are not true (10:300) and a dissimulator who composes his face in a way that seems appropriate for the interviews he is about to have (10:293, 300). His cynicism and his Machiavellian exaltation of means over ends are slyly noted by Stavrogin: As "a realist," Stavrogin says, Peter "cannot lie" and "truth is more precious to him than success . . . except, of course, in those special cases when success is more precious than truth" (10:156). Like Nechaev again, Peter believes in the power of form. He has introduced uniforms – for which Nechaev had a fondness – and busily devises ranks and duties: He has "secretaries, secret spies, treasurers, chairmen, registrars and their assistants" (10:298). Finally, it is a socialism of a totalitarian sort that Peter, like Nechaev, seems to envisage. Nechaev apparently believed that a juridical system could be devised that would force people to be equal⁹ and envisaged the concentration of all power in the hands of a "committee" that would compel citizens to work according to their capabilities and would withhold the means of livelihood from them if they did not comply.[10] Peter, for his part, expresses admiration for the authoritarian Russian administration, "the only thing in Russia that is natural and attained" (10:180).

In a more general way, too, *The Devils* mirrors the upsurge of revolutionary feeling in the Russian intelligentsia in the late 1860s and the increased organizational and agitational activity among the radical youth. For the novel re-creates the world of the revolutionary underground, a world of secret societies and cells, assumed identities and secret signs (10:437), safe houses and false documents (10:322), clandestine printing presses, codes of rules (10:298), spies and *agents provocateurs*, student disorders, industrial unrest, incendiarism, and talk of brigandage and elemental peasant revolt. In particular, it is punctuated by reference to agitational literature of the sort that had caused so much alarm in reality. Proclamations begin to appear in the province (10:248) and turn up at a nearby garrison and at the local Shpigulin factory (10:269). Peter discusses examples of the genre with Karmazinov (10:287) and even with von Lembke, who turns out to have a personal collection of these proclamations, Russian and foreign, accumulated since 1859 (10:245). At the top of one is a drawing of an axe, a fearsome symbol of the threatened revolutionary violence familiar from P. G. Zaichnevsky's leaflet "Young Russia,"[11] and reappearing in the oval seal of Nechaev's Committee of the People's Revenge. Yet another proclamation on von Lembke's desk, entitled "A Radiant Personality," supposedly written by Herzen in honor of Shatov and emanating from a foreign press (10:273, 276), parodies a poem actually written by Ogarev, entitled "The Student" and dedicated, at Bakunin's suggestion, to Nechaev. Virginskaia's younger sister, a student from St. Petersburg, has several hundred copies of a leaflet that she has written herself (10:304). Copies of a further proclamation are planted on Stepan Verkhovensky, presumably by his son (10:331), and later Peter produces yet another proclamation which he instructs Liputin to have printed after Shatov's murder (10:424).[12]

Furthermore, most of the sections of the Russian population that were identified by revolutionaries as promising objects for their attention come within the purview of Peter Verkhovensky and the members of his society or their sympathizers. Students in the higher educational institutions are exhorted by Virginskaia's sister, during the hysterical scenes at the fête, to rise up in protest at their sufferings (10:375). Indeed, the young woman is en route to university towns in the hope of stirring up student disturbances (10:304). Soldiers of a regiment stationed locally show signs of atheism and encourage Peter Verkhovensky to believe that they will support the movement (10:180, 315). The workers at the Shpigulin factory, which is a breeding ground for cholera and where workers are being laid off (10:180), begin to complain when the manager cheats them of the wages due to them (10:269–70) and eventually about seventy of their number assemble outside the governor's residence.[13]

There is the threat, too, of the elemental peasant rebellion, or *bunt*, that it was the objective of Bakunin and his followers to precipitate. Like Bakunin, who was probably responsible for that part of the "Catechism of a Revolutionary" which urged a search for means to "drive the *narod* [i.e., the people] beyond the limits of its patience" and incite an "all-shattering revolution,"[14] Peter Verkhovensky finds the idea of "destruction" alluring. He hopes by such forms of agitation as rumor and arson to generate a violent revolt like those that had periodically erupted in Russia in the seventeenth and eighteenth centuries and that continued to echo in more localized peasant uprisings in the nineteenth century. At the head of this *bunt* Peter plans to install a figure like Stenka Razin (10:201), the Cossack Bakunin so admired who had led the peasant rebellion of 1670–71, and it is for this purpose that he cultivates Stavrogin, who he thinks will serve as a charismatic leader. Even the phenomenon of brigandage (*razboinichestvo*), which Bakunin held up as "one of the worthiest forms of Russian folk life,"[15] an expression of the continuing existence of a free rebellious spirit among the common people, finds an echo in the novel in the person of Fedka, an escaped convict whom Peter considers of use in his schemes, and in the rumors of roving brigands that trouble Stepan Verkhovensky as he begins his final wandering (10:481).

There are even signs in the novel of the tensions that were developing in the revolutionary camp, partly as a result of the activities of Nechaev himself. These tensions take the form of differences of opinion within Peter Verkhovensky's secret society over such matters as the organization of the society, the nature of the revolution it hopes to carry out, and the character of the society that it would introduce on the morrow of the revolution. First, the choice between peaceful propaganda, as recommended by P. L. Lavrov's followers, and violent *bunt*, as recommended by Bakunin's followers, is proposed by the lame teacher in the debate at Virginsky's (10:314). Second, the qualms felt by the anarchic majority of Russian socialists about hierarchical revolutionary organization – qualms that came to the surface following the trial of the *Nechaevtsy* – are reflected in the fact that at least three members of the cell of five, alarmed by the turn of events in the town (arson, the murder of Lebiadkin and his sister and maid, and the violence done to Liza Tushina) and irritated by Peter Verkhovensky's late arrival for a secret meeting with them, wonder whether to disband the cell and form a new secret society for the "propaganda of ideas" on the principles of democracy and equal rights (10:415–16). Third, the preoccupation of that same anarchic majority with social and economic transformation rather than seizure of political power and a naive faith that revolution could somehow be effected from below without attention to political institutions are reflected in Virginsky's regret, recorded by the narrator in his conclusion, at the "political" turn that the movement has taken, its deviation from the "social" path (10:511).

2. Russian Liberalism

The content of "liberalism" in Russia in Dostoevsky's lifetime should not be too closely identified with the ideology implied by the term in the nineteenth century in relation to Western European countries in general and to Victorian England in particular. In fact, the term was often loosely used, as when Dostoevsky himself spoke of the "mangy Russian liberalism" which induced him in the 1840s to associate himself with the *Petrashevtsy* (see introduction, page 37). When the term did have more specific meaning, it still did not as rule denote the enthusiasm characteristic of Western liberals for laissez-faire economics or a desire to reduce the state's role in the life of the individual. Rather, it indicated an aspiration to introduce into Russia elements of what was regarded as the superior civilization of Western Europe. This development would, in all probability, have to be overseen in Russia by the autocratic state itself in order to ensure stability. Liberals in Russia, therefore, stood for gradual, peaceful, limited reform of the country, evolutionary change from above rather than revolutionary upheaval either in the form of peasant revolt from below or "Jacobin" coup d'état carried out by a revolutionary minority over the heads of the masses. "Liberalism" is primarily associated in mid-nineteenth-century Russia with sections of the nobility and officialdom rather than with an entrepreneurial bourgeoisie, which, in any case, did not at that time exist as a coherent class.

As such, "liberals" met with opposition from both the more radical Westernist intelligentsia from which the revolutionary movement eventually issued and from thinkers like Dostoevsky himself who belonged to the conservative nationalist stream of Russian thought. They are associated by both camps with effete posturing, empty rhetoric, and hypocritical advocacy of high-sounding ideals that they are allegedly not prepared fully to translate into practice. Liberalism, complained Chernyshevsky, conceived freedom "in a very narrow, formal way," as an "abstract right, as permission on paper" but without an understanding that "legal permission only has any value for a man when he has the material means to take advantage of this permission."[16] The tendency attributed to liberals to take themselves seriously and to create an impression of useful activity while making little progress is ridiculed in *The Devils* in the literary quadrille at the end of the fête: The figure representing the newspaper *The Voice*, a liberal organ that came out in St. Petersburg from 1863 to 1883, dances with a solid expression on his face, taking quick little steps but hardly moving from the spot and emitting moderate sounds in a deep, hoarse voice (10:389). The revolutionary case against liberal gradualism is expressed forcefully in the novel by Peter Verkhovensky in an argument with the lame teacher at the gathering at Virginsky's. To chatter in an eloquent liberal way is very pleasant, as Peter impatiently says, but Russians who desire change face a simple choice: whether to cross the swamp – a favorite image for stagnant Russia among the radical intelligentsia – at the pace of a tortoise or at full steam (10:315–16).

The principal representative of liberalism in *The Devils* is Stepan Verkhovensky. He is linked to a distinguished cluster of figures from the older generation: At one time his name had been mentioned along with those of P. Ia. Chaadaev, V. G. Belinsky, T. N. Granovsky, and Herzen (10:8). It is at a dinner in Moscow in honor of Granovsky that he and Karmazinov, who on one level represents a scathing attack by Dostoevsky on the novelist Turgenev, last met (10:348). Indeed, it is with Granovsky himself that Stepan Verkhovensky, through biographical details and personal traits, is most closely linked. Granovsky (1813–1855), professor of world history at the University of Moscow throughout the 1840s, was the leading moderate Westernizer of his generation, whose public lectures of 1843–44 on medieval European history, delivered in the dark age of Nicholas I (ruled from 1825 to 1855), won him great acclaim.[17] The first chapter of *The Devils* is packed with implicit reference to Granovsky's life, work, interests, and personality, the information on which is partly culled from a biography of Granovsky compiled by A. V. Stankevich and published in 1869.[18] Writing from Dresden early in 1870, at the time when *The Devils* was being conceived, Dostoevsky begged his friend N. N. Strakhov to send him this book (Dostoevsky uses the pejorative form *knizhonka* in his letter) which he urgently needed as essential, indispensable material for his novel (29/i:111).

Like Granovsky, who studied at Berlin in the 1830s, Stepan Verkhovensky has spent some time abroad in his youth and has shone at the university lectern in the late 1840s. His "brilliant dissertation" on the German town of Hanau and its relations with the Hanseatic League in the early fifteenth century (10:8) brings to mind Granovsky's own master's dissertation on two medieval Baltic townships and the magnificent mythical city of Vineta which popular imagination and later historiography located beneath the sea off the Pomeranian coast.[19] Granovsky's dissertation was felt to be critical of the Slavophiles inasmuch as its dismissal of the legend of Vineta was perceived as implying rejection of equally romantic Slavophile notions about Russia's past that had no basis in historical fact. Similarly, Stepan Verkhovensky's dissertation has piqued the Slavophiles and won him implacable enemies among them (10:8–9). Stepan Verkhovensky's research "on the causes of the exceptional moral nobility of certain knights-errant" (10:9) and the "Tales from Spanish History" (10:61; see also 235) with which he hopes to reassert himself in Russian intellectual life echo Granovsky's passion for the subject of chivalry, a passion apparent in an article on the late-fifteenth- and early-sixteenth-century French knight Pierre Terrail de Bayard, the knight "*sans peur et sans reproche*," and in a late essay on the Castilian hero celebrated in the epic *El Cid*.[20] The spirit of chivalry is expressed, too, in Stepan's reverence for women – Varvara Stavrogina, Daria Shatova, Sofia Ulitina – whom he seems to see himself as serving in a quixotic way. Stepan is also prone, like Granovsky, to bouts of melancholy (10:12) and shares the historian's passion for gambling (10:12, 45–47).

However, the enlightened Westernism and civilized sensibility commonly attributed to Granovsky are portrayed by Dostoevsky, through his blundering, ingenuous narrator, in an unflattering light. Stepan's quixotism is presented as vacuous: The narrator, unable to give a positive answer, forbears to reply to Stepan's rhetorical question as to whether he, Stepan, faced with Varvara Stavrogina's proposal that he marry Daria Shatova, has enough moral strength to walk out when "honor and the great principle of independence" demand it (10:73). There is a strong hint of cowardice (*malodushie*) in Stepan's conduct (10:264). Moreover, what is held up as an achievement on Stepan's part is immediately qualified. He is a man of science but, in truth, has produced almost nothing and his career at the lectern has been extremely brief. Of his profound examination of knight-errantry, only the beginning exists and the most probable explanation of his failure to complete it is simply indolence (10:8–9). His fulfillment of a civic role in his community is histrionic; indeed the narrator himself compares Stepan Verkhovensky to "an actor at the theater" (10:7). This impression is confirmed when Stepan prepares for his speech at the fête by rehearsing in front of a mirror and garnering for the occasion all the witticisms and puns he has noted down in a little exercise book (10:353). Stepan revels in the position of someone persecuted, an exile, but it emerges that, in fact, he has never been in exile or even under official surveillance (10:7–8). Far from being a useful citizen, then, Stepan needs a listener with whom he can share a bottle of champagne and to whom he can deliver his ideas about Russia, the "Russian spirit," and the "Russian God" (10:30). Thus the ideal of noble, altruistic service as it had been constructed by the "men of the 1840s" is presented instead as the selfish need of an immature personality – the narrator stresses Stepan's childish quality (10:35) – to parade and attract attention to itself.

At first sight the "liberal of the 1840s," whom Stepan Verkhovensky represents and as Liamshin characterizes him (10:252), might seem to have little more than historical or comic relevance in the new climate of Russia after the Crimean War. After all, in the 1860s Stepan Verkhovensky seems first "forgotten" and "unnecessary" (10:20) and then, after his fame has briefly flickered again (he is mentioned in the foreign press, then as a former star in a famous constellation and for some reason even compared to A. N. Radishchev [10:20]),[21] he seems distinctly *passé*. He suffers a fiasco in St. Petersburg where, despite his willingness to deride the word "fatherland" and to proclaim the harmfulness of religion, he has the temerity to oppose the nihilists' view that a cobbler is more valuable than a great artist and therefore to insist that "boots are inferior to Pushkin" (10:23). And yet, as Richard Peace has pointed out, *The Devils* takes up the theme of the relationship between generations which had been explored most notably by Turgenev in *Fathers and Sons*[22] and, on this level, the question of the degree of responsibility borne by the "men of the 1840s" for the apocalypse which the "men of the 1860s" threaten to precipitate cannot be evaded.

As usual in Dostoevsky's fiction, a sin of omission is in evidence. For it can be held against Stepan Verkhovensky, as it will be against Fedor Karamazov in Dostoevsky's last novel, that he is a neglectful parent, a fact for which he expresses maudlin regret (10:101). He has only ever seen his son twice before the main action of the novel (10:161), most recently nine years previously (10:62), and, when Peter finally appears in person, Stepan does not at first recognize him (10:144). Peter himself reproaches his father for never having spent a ruble on him, for not knowing him at all until he was sixteen, and for hypocritically claiming that his heart had been bleeding for him all his life (10:240).

Acceptance of more direct responsibility, blame for sins of commission, Stepan Verkhovensky long resists. He rejects paternity of nihilism, lamenting that the "great idea" of his generation has been taken up by idiots, dragged into the streets, and displayed in the secondhand market in an unrecognizable form (10:24) and, later, again accusing the young of grossly distorting that idea (10:238). Yet, the very structure of *The Devils*, which begins with a sustained portrayal of the liberal Westernizer of the 1840s, leads us to believe that it is in the corrosive free thinking of men like Stepan Verkhovensky that the profound moral and ultimately existential problems addressed by the novel have their roots. In any case, Stepan Verkhovensky is in one way or another the progenitor of both the monsters who stand at the center of the novel (and who are artistically yoked together, inasmuch as Peter Verkhovensky, without Stavrogin, is like "a fly, an idea without a phial, Columbus without America" [10:324]). Peter Verkhovensky, the son born to Stepan by his first wife, a flighty local girl from whom he had soon separated and who had died in Paris when the child was five (10:11), is, of course, Stepan's blood descendant. At the same time Stavrogin, the son of Varvara Stavrogina with whom Stepan Verkhovensky has been living in an apparently Platonic relationship for some twenty years when the novel begins, is his moral and cultural creation. For Stepan has been responsible for Stavrogin's education both in the sense of moral upbringing (*vospitanie*) and intellectual development (*umstvennoe razvitie*) (10:10). The point is so important that it is repeated in chapter 2 (10:35). We may note that the unstable Liza Tushina, too, was a pupil of Stepan's from the age of eight to eleven (10:59). Von Lembke, knowing that Stepan Verkhovensky has been a tutor in the Stavrogin household, calls him the hotbed of everything that has now sprung up (10:345). More damning still, as the militant seminarist points out during Stepan's reading at the fête, the escaped convict Fedka might not now be robbing and killing in the locality had Stepan Verkhovensky not handed him over for military service fifteen years earlier in order to pay off a gambling debt (10:373). There is even a grotesque grain of allegorical truth in Peter Verkhovensky's impudent assertion that the fathers of families are to blame for the pandemonium of the fête inasmuch as they have failed to restrain the scoundrels there (10:382).

However, it is not only Stepan Verkhovensky who is, in some degree, responsible through "liberalism" for the nihilist contagion now afflicting Russia. For there is a more general tendency on the part of the older generation of the educated class to conduct a dangerous flirtation with the revolutionary youth. Thus, among the throng who gather at Varvara Stavrogina's when she visits St. Petersburg in the early 1860s, there appear a few older literary celebrities of undoubted distinction, some of whom shamefully try to ingratiate themselves with the new riff-raff (10:21). Within the main body of the novel Julia von Lembke – to whom the narrator attributes much of the responsibility for the events of the dénouement (10:248) – deludes herself that through Peter Verkhovensky she can exercise an influence on the whole revolutionary youth of Russia. By this means, she will avert the revolutionary catastrophe threatening the country and earn herself the acclaim of Russian liberalism (10:247–48, 268, 339). Varvara Stavrogina, not to be outdone by her social rival, also begins to parrot the views of the young (for which she is accused by Stepan Verkhovensky of selling her freedom for a mess of pottage [10:263]). The writer Karmazinov – a distant relation of Julia von Lembke and once a friend of Stepan Verkhovensky (10:70) – also sucks up to the radical youth in a way that is demeaning, considering that they pay him scant attention (10:170, 284), despite his condescension toward others who do not belong to the highest echelons of society (10:70). Von Lembke himself acquiesces in undermining the state he serves when he tries to persuade Peter that it is premature to introduce radical change (a classic liberal position) but seems not to argue that churches should never be destroyed. While he affirms that officialdom, which must concern itself with the decent appearance of things, will sometimes have to keep the young within certain bounds, he encourages Peter to seek progress and even to undermine things that are obsolete. He thinks officialdom and the radical youth are mutually necessary, like the English Tories and Whigs (10:246).

Thus, in the persons of Stepan Verkhovensky, Julia von Lembke, Karmazinov, and Andrei von Lembke, liberalism finds support in several spheres: former academic life, polite society, belles-lettres, and even the government apparatus. Indeed, it has spread more widely still, as we are reminded when Peter Verkhovensky outlines to Stavrogin the extent of the support on which his secret society may count. The society, he argues, embraces not merely those who kill, burn, fire off pistols, or bite but also those whom we might now call fellow travelers: the teacher who laughs with his pupils at God, the barrister who defends an educated client who has murdered less-developed people for money, the schoolboys who kill a peasant for the thrill of it, jurors who invariably acquit defendants, administrators, men of letters (10:324). All such types are, in a sense, complicit in the revolutionary destruction that is being planned and is even now beginning and all will be ruthlessly exploited by revolutionaries of the sort described in Nechaev's "Catechism,"[23] to whose outlook we shall now turn.

3. Nihilism

The outlook of the radical young generation is subsumed under the convenient label "nihilism." It is as "nihilism" that the socialist rebellion against the established values of "liberalism" manifests itself in Russia in the 1860s. At the core of nihilism, as it is presented by Dostoevsky in *The Devils*, lay unnatural views on art and human aspirations and a repudiation of nationality which, when pushed to their logical extremes – and Dostoevsky loved to push ideas to their logical extremes – turned out to prescribe slavery or death. However, before turning to these essential properties of nihilism we should note, first, the literary resonance of Dostoevsky's polemic with it and, second, his observation of such externals as nihilist manners, demeanor, and attitudes.

As a critique of nihilism *The Devils* belongs, up to a point, to a seam of Russian literature exemplified by the antinihilist novels of A. F. Pisemsky, N. S. Leskov, and others.[24] Running parallel to the tradition of the antinihilist novel is another seam, exemplified by works by A. V. Sleptsov, D. L. Mordovstev, I. V. Omulevsky, and I. A. Kushchevsky, in which the potential revolutionary, the "positive hero" who supplants the inert "superfluous man" associated with the age of Nicholas I, is extolled.[25] At the fountainhead of this latter tradition stands Chernyshevsky's *What Is to Be Done?* (1863), in which the leader of the radical intelligentsia gave fictional expression, among other things, to his faith in the possibility of applying scientific method to all human problems, his ethical doctrine of rational egoism,[26] his view of the family as a prison, his vision of future social forms based on cooperation, and his plea for the emancipation of woman.

The Devils repeatedly engages with *What Is to Be Done?* Dostoevsky appears to be scoffing at Chernyshevsky's views on the subject of marriage and free love when he reports a story that Virginsky, on learning that his wife was dismissing him, told her that he not only loved her but now respected her as well (10:29). Stepan Verkhovensky, preparing for a decisive confrontation with the "shriekers" of the young generation, is making a careful study of Chernyshevsky's novel in order to know their methods and arguments from their "catechism" itself (10:238). The utopia with "columns of aluminum" to which Shigalev dismissively refers (10:311) is that dreamed of by Chernyshevsky's Vera Pavlovna and modeled on that apotheosis of nineteenth-century technological progress, the Crystal Palace.[27] Maria Shatova, in her plan to set up a bookbinding enterprise "on rational principles of association" (10:441), seems to be aping Vera Pavlovna, who establishes a cooperative of seamstresses. Rational egoism is perhaps parodied in the suggestion that Shatov set Maria at odds with the family in which she was a governess with the egoistic aim of marrying her (10:449). Stavrogin's marriage to Maria Lebiadkina may be seen as an absurd extension of the practice of marrying for magnanimous ends, as exemplified by the union of Lopukhov, one of Chernyshevsky's "new people," with Vera Pavlovna, in order that she be freed from domestic tyranny. There are even grounds for seeing Stavrogin, the supremely willful being, as a macabre reworking of Chernyshevsky's "salt of the earth," Rakhmetov. One is reminded of Rakhmetov's practice of testing his will by lying on a bed of nails when Stavrogin, having been struck by Shatov, resists the temptation to take his vengeance by killing him on the spot – which is what the narrator is convinced he will do – and instead places his arms behind his back like a person who has seized a red-hot piece of iron and gripped it for ten seconds to test his firmness by overcoming the unbearable pain (10:166).

Turning from possible literary echoes in *The Devils* to Dostoevsky's own presentation of the nihilist persona, we find that, on a superficial level, nihilism manifests itself in conduct of the same sort that Turgenev, so viciously lampooned in the character of Karmazinov, had carefully observed in *Fathers and Sons*. Peter Verkhovensky, like Turgenev's Bazarov but to a much greater degree, has the free manner, and disdain for manners, characteristic of a generation that rejects the formal civilities of its elders. He is over-familiar, insolent, strews insults at his father (10:237–39), uses coarse language (10:172), and abuses hospitality (the governor comes home one day to find him sleeping uninvited in his study [10:244]). He has the impudent habit of lolling on chairs and sofas and tucking his feet up under him (10:238, 272). He despises honor, an aristocratic concept dear to the older generation. To his father's fury he derides friendship – cherished by the "men of the 1840s" – as a "mutual outpouring of slops" (10:263). Like the revolutionary depicted in Nechaev's "Catechism," whose relations with another person are determined solely by the degree of his usefulness in the revolutionary cause,[28] Peter bases his own relationships on political calculation. Thus he cynically uses Julia von Lembke for his own ends (10:510–11), having ingratiated himself with her "by means of the coarsest flattery" (10:379).

At a deeper level, the radicals as a whole tend not to exhibit warmth or what the narrator considers natural human feelings in their attitudes toward and relationships with others.[29] Virginskaia's sister, who speaks in clichés, argues violently about the "woman question" with her uncle, whom she has not seen for ten years and who had carried her in his arms when she was a baby (10:304, 306). Maria Shatova rejects compassion and curses her child before it is born (10:442–43). And whereas to Shatov the birth of Maria's child – of which he is not the father – evokes awe at the miraculous appearance of a new, third spirit where before there were only two, the midwife Virginskaia, having delivered the baby, describes human birth as merely the "further development of the organism," an event no more mysterious than the birth of a fly. To her the paramount consideration to which birth gives rise is social: Conditions need to be changed so that superfluous people are not born who will have to be handed over to homes for foundlings (10:452).[30] The emotional abnormality attributed by Dostoevsky to nihilists seems also to be manifested in their casual or destructive attitude toward the institutions of marriage and the family. The radical intelligentsia of the time expected to replace marriage with free love and the family with cooperatives or communes of the sort envisaged by Chernyshevsky in *What Is to Be Done?* and exemplified in reality by forms of corporate life that were widespread among the student population. Likewise, in *The Devils* Shatov's wife Maria abandons him after less than three weeks (10:27, 434); Virginsky's wife, Arina Prokhorovna, informs him after less than a year that he is "dismissed" and takes up with Lebiadkin instead (10:29); and Virginskaia's sister speculates on the origin of people's irrational "prejudice" about the sanctity of the institution of the family (10:306).

The lack of respect and love for fellow human beings, which seem in *The Devils* to underlie nihilists' human relationships, are of a piece with their views on art, to which there is persistent reference in the novel. That the subject of aesthetics should have importance in a novel that focuses on the nascent revolutionary movement is not so surprising as it might seem at first. For discussion of art had an emblematic significance in mid-nineteenth-century Russia. It was the first battleground for debate between the liberal and socialist wings of the Westernist intelligentsia. Among the radical intelligentsia it was commonplace from the mid-1850s, when Chernyshevsky published his influential dissertation on "The Aesthetic Relationship of Art to Reality,"[31] to assert that art at its best reproduced reality and that it should be valued in proportion to its utility in serving the goals of science, progress, and social improvement. To Dostoevsky, on the other hand, art had a central place in man's moral life. Great works of art, unconstrained by the requirements of a particular faction in a given time and place, transcended mundane reality and wrought immeasurable spiritual improvement in mankind as a whole.[32]

In *The Devils* there are frequent echoes of this controversy. The nihilists' utilitarian view of art is encapsulated in remarks made by, or attributed to, several characters on the subject of Raphael's Sistine Madonna, housed in a gallery at Dresden. Raphael's painting exemplifies the art rejected by the radicals and by those who, for one reason or another, fall in with them. It is a source of bitter dispute between the Verkhovenskys, father and son disagreeing over the proposition that it is less useful than carts of grain (10:172). Julia von Lembke, basking in her apparent cultural preeminence over Varvara Stavrogina, opines that enthusiasm for the painting is outmoded: She says she has come away from the painting disillusioned, having sat in front of it for two hours, and claims that Karmazinov endorses her opinion (10:235). Varvara Stavrogina later parrots this opinion to Stepan Verkhovensky and embroiders it with banalities which echo Chernyshevsky's thesis that art is a "surrogate" for reality. A mug is useful, she patronizingly explains to Stepan, because one can pour water into it; a pencil is useful because one can write things down with it; but the Madonna serves no purpose. No one confronted with a real apple and a drawing of it will take the latter (10:264).[33]

To Dostoevsky this crabbed view of art is an indication of the nihilists' failure to understand man's eternal aesthetic – and therefore spiritual – needs. He polemicizes with it through Stepan Verkhovensky, whose status rises toward the end of the novel. Stepan plans to use his appearance at the fête to defend the divine countenance of a great ideal which the young are tearing up in the name of equality, envy, and the digestion (10:265–66). (The nihilists' preoccupation with the most basic material needs at the expense of man's spiritual aspirations had long dismayed Dostoevsky: Socialists, he had pronounced in his notebooks in the mid-1860s, went no further than the belly (20:192).) At the fête itself he identifies differing conceptions of beauty as the core of the disagreement between the intolerant younger generation and his own. It is a choice, as he memorably puts it, between Shakespeare and shoes, Raphael and petroleum. For Stepan Verkhovensky Shakespeare and Raphael are superior to the emancipation of the serfs, nationality, socialism, the younger generation, or chemistry, for they are the highest achievements of mankind, the fruit of the quest for beauty, the only thing people cannot live without on Earth (10:372–73). This insistence on art as a vehicle for a transcendent beauty toward which free people restlessly strive is directly related to Stepan's final rediscovery of Christian truths and his assertion on his deathbed that if people are deprived of the "immeasurably great," they will cease to live and will die in despair (10:506).

Those who deny people's aspiration toward something higher than their physical being and whose gaze is fixed on the material world alone pin all their hopes on reason and on what in the nineteenth century seemed reason's outstanding accomplishment, natural science. Exalted by Chernyshevsky and Pisarev as providing a method applicable to all problems, even aesthetic, moral, social, and political problems, science underpinned a crude materialism that eroded and even replaced religious belief. In *The Devils* this development is attested by the young second lieutenant in a nearby garrison who sets out the works of Vogt, Moleschott, and Büchner (three German materialist thinkers who exercised a considerable influence on Russian radical thought in the late 1850s and 1860s) on lecterns and burns church candles in front of them (10:269). Natural science and the view of human beings promoted by narrow advocacy of it also underlie Shigalev's rejection of all previous utopian designs – including those of Fourier, who inspired the *Petrashevtsy*, and Chernyshevsky himself, as well as Plato and Rousseau – as the fantasies of foolish dreamers. His own "final solution" to the problem of reconciling the desire for limitless freedom with the desire for equality has an exemplary mathematical tidiness about it. Adumbrated in ten chapters, it divides mankind into two parts, one-tenth of which will enjoy complete freedom of personality and unbounded rights over the remaining nine-tenths, who will be transformed through coercion into an obedient herd (10:311–12).[34] It is appropriate that Shigalev should describe his blueprint for the rigorously planned society of the future at a gathering at a house located on Ant Street (*Murav'inaia ulitsa;* 10:300). For the ant hill, the habitat of eusocial insects that appear to have rationally ordered their existence in a collective spirit, is accepted by radical thinkers as a fitting symbol of utopia in a scientific age.[35]

It should be added, finally, that beyond the political and social nihilism manifested in revolutionary activity and in rejection of existing codes of conduct, attitudes, and aesthetic values, there lies in the dislocated world that Dostoevsky observes a profound moral nihilism which in *The Devils* finds its fullest expression in the person of Stavrogin (see the introduction, pages 42–54). Pisarev, writing about Turgenev's nihilist Bazarov, had remarked that the actions of individuals who acknowledge no regulator, moral law, or principle outside themselves are governed merely by circumstances and personal taste. Such individuals might turn out to be "civic dignitaries" or "inveterate swindlers," pioneering scientists and public servants, or robbers and murderers.[36] In Stavrogin, Dostoevsky offers his own portrayal of a man who, in the absence of a moral core, is unable to distinguish aesthetically between a bestial voluptuous act and some spiritual exploit such as the sacrifice of one's life for the benefit of mankind (10:201). Such a man falls back on continual existential experimentation with various personae. Thus Stavrogin repudiates the universal language of the social republic and harmony (10:45) and yet becomes a member of Peter Verkhovensky's "society." Alongside a proud Byronism there coexists in him a tendency to descend into a terrible "Sodom" (10:149). He undertakes an apparently quixotic defense of Lebiadkina which is presented as the fantasy of a world-weary man or even a "new étude by a sated man with the object of discovering how far one could push a mad cripple" (10:150). Again, it is Stavrogin who has originally convinced Shatov of a people's need for life-affirming religion, and yet at the very same time he has been filling Kirillov's heart with thoughts of death (10:196–97). Stavrogin, then, amounts to a monstrous caricature of the rational egoism which Russian radical thought in the 1860s took as its ethical base: Even though he is coldly rational (10:165), his pleasure is derived not exclusively from acts of general utility but indiscriminately from both good and evil acts (10:514).

4. Loss of Nationality

Already in the publicism he produced after his return from Siberian exile, Dostoevsky had expressed anxiety about the obliteration of national distinctions. In polemical articles directed at Chernyshevsky in the early 1860s he had castigated those who sought a man "who would be everywhere one and the same – in Germany, in England, or in France, who would embody that common type of man that has been produced in the West."[37] The specter of the "universal man" (*obshchechelovek*) continues to haunt Dostoevsky in *The Devils* (the term is actually applied to Virginsky; 10:177). In proportion to their becoming citizens of the world, so the affinity of educated Russians with their native soil, the concept of *pochva* on which Dostoevsky's political thought is founded, is weakened. This dissociation, in the extreme form in which Dostoevsky thinks he observes it, entails not only a more or less passive loss of association with ethnic roots but also a more extreme and active "splitting off from consciousness of certain ideas and their accompanying emotions," to use a modern definition of the term.[38] However, it is not exclusively the radical camp that exhibits a dangerous dissociation from its native soil. In this respect liberals and nihilists, for all their points of difference, converge in *The Devils*. For example, both groups are presented in one of Shatov's diatribes as fearing their own independence and as being lackeys of thought, enemies of personality and freedom (10:442). Both "men of the 1840s" and "men of the 1860s" are Westernizers of a sort and both these sets of characters in *The Devils* ape foreign ways and fall into the habit of assuming that their own culture is inferior to that of Western Europe.

Within the liberal camp Stepan Verkhovensky, who considers himself truly Russian (10:78, 171–72) and claims to be an expert on Russia and the Russian people (10:76–77), cannot make any substantial utterance without including a French phrase. He thinks that Russians do not know how to say anything in their own language, or at least have not said anything till now (10:51). He makes well-meaning but patronizing remarks about the Russian people that demonstrate both his distance from them and sense of superiority to them: He thinks the Russian peasant has been brought into fashion by the intelligentsia, which has produced a branch of imaginative literature on the subject and placed "laurel wreaths on heads covered in lice" (10:31). He flatters himself that he knows how to communicate with the common people (10:486), but to the peasants who offer him a ride in their cart he is an alien being (10:482). Karmazinov is in the process of moving abroad altogether, ostensibly because the climate is better there and the buildings are made of stone, but also because he sees Russia, of all the countries in the world, as the one most susceptible to revolutionary propaganda – a view apparently shared by socialists internationally (10:314) – and does not believe Russia is capable of withstanding the approaching revolutionary wave. In any case he seems to despise Russia: It is a wooden, destitute country, doomed and without a future. He has become a German and is proud of it (10:287). The question of the new sewage system which is to be constructed in Karlsruhe, where he has been living for seven years, is dearer to him than all the questions of his sweet fatherland over the whole reform period (10:349). In his speech at the fête he seems to the narrator to be laughing at Russia, taking pleasure in declaring it bankrupt in all respects before the great minds of Europe (10:367). Julia von Lembke, maliciously guffawing at her husband's reproaches for her liaison with Peter Verkhovensky, is compared to a Parisian actress hired at colossal expense to play a certain role (10:340). As for Andrei von Lembke, he is a Russian of German extraction, a member of an alien official caste, and his foreignness is stressed, with an underlying tone of hostility, in the lengthy portrait that Dostoevsky provides in the middle of the novel (10:241–43).[39]

The radical camp, like Stepan Verkhovensky, appears to take an interest in the popular masses. However, it is an interest that is based on an equally false preconception as to the peasant's nature – in this case, that the masses are not so much charming as mutinous – and is accordingly disparaged by Dostoevsky. Perhaps it is as a gibe against the enthusiasm of the radical intelligentsia of the 1860s for minute observation of the people's way of life, history, movements, and sufferings[40] that Dostoevsky frames Shatov's remark to the effect that a people that loses its distinctive conception of God and ceases to believe that it alone bears the truth becomes "mere ethnographic material" (10:199–200). Elsewhere in the novel poets without talent who affect peasant dress are included in the narrator's venomous list of types who have achieved preeminence in the contemporary intelligentsia (10:354). Most important, Tolkachenko, one of the members of Peter Verkhovensky's revolutionary cell, is rather obviously modeled on Pryzhov (see section I, above), who was famed for the study he had made of the dregs of Russian society and for his book on the taverns (*kabaki*) of Russia.[41] Dostoevsky cannot resist negative strokes in Tolkachenko's portrait, underlining his alcoholism and treating his donning of shabby clothes and his use of peasant phraseology as forms of exhibitionism (10:302, 512).

Behind the interest the radical camp professes in the lower depths of Russian life lies the same dissociation from native soil that is apparent in the liberal camp. To Shatov, the nihilists exhibit an animal hatred of Russia that has eaten into their organism (10:111). To Stepan Verkhovensky, at the height of his arguments with his son, they seem to denigrate the Russians as revolting parasites who are idle and incapable of producing any idea and who should be exterminated for the good of mankind (10:172). Even the educated *barich*[42] Stavrogin has not quite mastered the art of writing in his native language, and his final letter to Daria Shatova, mischievously reproduced verbatim by the narrator in the closing pages of the novel, contains linguistic mistakes (10:513). It is because he is bound by nothing in Russia (10:513) – indeed, he has become a citizen of the Swiss canton of Uri – that he is neither hot nor cold but exhibits that lukewarm quality for which St. John the Divine berates the Laodicean Church (10:497) in the Book of Revelation to which reference in *The Devils* is so pervasive. The inclusion in Peter Verkhovensky's secret society of the Jew Liamshin – in whose depiction we glimpse Dostoevsky's anti-Semitism and who is discredited in the novel by his participation in idiotic japes such as the planting of obscene photographs in the pedlar Sofia Ulitina's bag of Bibles – further underlines the alien nature of the nihilist dementia.

However, it is perhaps Kirillov who is most obviously divorced from his native soil and in whom the consequences of this dissociation are seen at their most extreme. According to Shatov – who shared with Kirillov the experience of living as a manual worker in America, but whose outlook has now radically changed – the two of them took the view that, as Russians, they were so inferior to the Americans that whatever they found in America they extolled, even spiritualism, lynch laws, guns, and tramps (10:112). Kirillov, like another copy from a foreign original, Lebeziatnikov in *Crime and Punishment*, speaks Russian awkwardly: He arranges words rather oddly and becomes muddled if he has to compose a longish sentence (10:75). The narrator even asks him why he does not speak Russian correctly and suggests that he has grown unused to the language during his five years abroad. Kirillov has no cogent answer to the question, is unaware that he speaks incorrectly, insists that he has spoken in the same way all his life, and is unperturbed by the fault the narrator has found (10:94). Lacking the moral landmarks that Dostoevsky associates with a strong sense of nationality, Kirillov stretches Panglossian optimism to its ultimate absurdity, claiming that all is good in the world, whether it be a person dying of hunger, a man violating a little girl, or someone smashing a child's head. Time has ended for him with this discovery, and he now awaits the moment when he will find godhood as a "new man" by overcoming fear of death through self-destruction (10:93–94).

The loss of national identity, like the loss of awareness of aesthetic and spiritual horizons beyond the material world, is associated by Dostoevsky with a view of life grounded in theory rather than reality. Thus, in his articles and notebooks of the early 1860s, alongside his remarks about the "universal man," we find reproachful references to "theoreticians" who survey life from their studies, "bend reality toward themselves,"[43] dwell "in the air, in complete isolation and without any support on the soil,"[44] and formulate ideas that are true "only on paper."[45] The same complaint informs, in particular, the portrayal of the radical camp in *The Devils*. The nihilists, in Shatov's words, are "paper people" (10:110, 112), "enemies of living life" (10:442). The ardent utopian socialist Liputin, who has on his table a volume of Considérant which he says is not so much a "translation from the French" as from "the language of the universal human social republic and harmony" and who dreams of the prospect of the establishment of a Fourierist phalanstery in Russia, overlooks the fact, as the narrator sees it in his more omniscient authorial vein, that there is not for a hundred miles around a single human being who remotely resembles the future member of the "universal all-human social republic and harmony" (10:44–45). Again, in the considered judgment of the inhabitants of the provincial town in which the novel is set, Peter Verkhovensky, although his talent for organization is admired, has proved himself completely ignorant of reality and is guilty of a terrible abstractness (*otvlechennost'*) that has brought about monstrous development in one direction only (10:512). Theory, then, may turn the world on its head. The socialism which may be paraded as philanthropy (e.g., 10:313) is, in fact, based on a hatred of mankind in the flesh, especially in its Russian manifestation.

5. Reconciliation on Native Soil

The Devils is pervaded by an air of impending catastrophe created by the many deaths by murder, suicide, and more or less natural causes, the conflagration that destroys part of the town as the fête is drawing to its conclusion, and the numerous references, implicit and explicit, to the Book of Revelation (see introduction, pages 38–42). At the same time, characters are driven by the hope of salvation in some form. To some, such as Shigalev and perhaps even Peter Verkhovensky, salvation seems to lie in the discovery of a new idea, new thought, or new word, the search for which obsessed the contemporary intelligentsia. Others – Shatov, Fedka, Lebiadkin, Maria Lebiadkina, perhaps Daria Shatova – pin their hopes on the enigmatic, protean Stavrogin. Kirillov claims to believe that he himself will save mankind through his expression of self-will (10:471–72). Julia von Lembke thinks she will save the entire young generation from themselves (10:268). Stepan Verkhovensky initially hopes for salvation at the hands of his son (10:101), but eventually it is the itinerant Bible pedlar Sofia Ulitina who becomes his "savior" (10:496). His last journey, which begins with no clear sense of purpose (10:480–

81), turns into a pilgrimage – never quite completed – to Spasov, a village named after the savior (Spas). As if to underline the importance of this goal, the name of the village occurs seventeen times in the first part of the chapter in question (10:484, 489–90). The questions we therefore need to ask, finally, are what evidence the novel furnishes of Dostoevsky's view as to where salvation lies and what hope it offers that such salvation might be achieved.

For Dostoevsky himself, as an exponent of *pochvennichestvo*, salvation was to be found in the rediscovery of a native God by the Westernized educated class, which had been thrown up by the reforms of Peter the Great, and in that class's reconciliation with the common people who had never lost their God. Such reconciliation required humble acceptance of simple Christian truths and of Christ in the Russian people's distinctive understanding of Him.

In his early publicism, inverting his opponents' arguments, Dostoevsky had asserted that Russians would only become universal men and attain the "ideal common to all mankind" when they brought into the sum of civilization their own special characteristics, that is, when they developed what was best and most distinctive in themselves.[46] In *The Devils* the mouthpiece for this view is Shatov who, it should be noted, is privileged in the Dostoevskian order of things by his intimacy with the lame simpleton Maria Lebiadkina,[47] by Maria's comparison of him with a monk (10:114), and even by the fact that he is relatively inarticulate.[48] No people, Shatov fervently explains, had ever ordered its life on the principles of science and reason extolled by socialists. On the contrary, science and reason would always play a secondary role, for people were moved by another force, the force of ceaseless confirmation of life and repudiation of death. This force, evoked in the scriptural image of "living fountains of waters" whose exhaustion is threatened in the Apocalypse, finds expression in a search for God in which every nation is engaged at every stage of its existence. God is not a universally uniform concept, however, but rather the distinctive "synthetic personality" of a people. Indeed, the distinctiveness of a people's God is for Shatov an indicator of that people's strength (10:198–99). Whereas the Western nations have lost God – Roman Catholicism, Shatov was once persuaded by Stavrogin, is not a form of Christianity (10:197) – the Russians are "God-bearers" who are uniquely capable of renewing and saving the world. They alone have been entrusted with the keys of a new life and the new word (10:196). Evidence that the Russians may indeed fulfill the destiny that Shatov outlines is of a largely negative kind in *The Devils*. At least nihilism proves self-defeating inasmuch as Kirillov and Stavrogin, like the Gadarene swine to whom the epigraph refers, destroy themselves, and Peter Verkhovensky, his revolutionary plans unfulfilled, is forced to flee abroad. Most encouraging is the doubt as to whether nihilism will ever gain the support it needs, if revolution is to be carried out, among the Russian people. Even the murderer Fedka, the incarnation of the *razboinichestvo* glorified by Bakunin, has a piety that makes him abhor Peter Verkhovensky as a pagan, an idolater, and a desecrator (10:428). Nor do the masses, as represented by the workers at the Shpigulin factory, show any revolutionary ardor.[49] While they do complain to the police about their treatment, they do so "without great clamor and without getting very excited about it" (10:270). Dostoevsky's narrator questions reports that have presented the demonstration outside von Lembke's residence as a *bunt* threatening the stability of the state and offers an alternative interpretation of it as a firm but peaceful protest, an instance of the old practice of the Russian people to go and have a chat with the "general himself" for the pleasure of it and without particular thought for the outcome. The credibility of claims that such demonstrations constitute expressions of popular socialist feeling is further undermined by the injection of an element of farce into the episode: Von Lembke, troubled by the disturbing turn of events in his domain and enraged by his wife's behavior, is suffering the beginnings of some mental derangement and arrives to confront the crowd, still clutching some flowers he has plucked in a field during an aimless ramble there (10:335–44).

More positive evidence of the possible reconciliation that Dostoevsky sought, however, is not altogether lacking in *The Devils*. It is furnished by the actions of Stepan Verkhovensky, the principal representative of the Russian intelligentsia with whom the novel has begun and who is redeemed in its closing pages. The need for reconciliation has dawned on Stepan before his final wandering, for in his speech at the fête he rebukes the nihilists for resisting it (10:373). Like Granovsky (who, in response to the materialism fanned by Feuerbach's *Essence of Christianity* and espoused by more radical Westernizers such as Herzen, could not abandon the concept of "some higher force"),[50] Stepan Verkhovensky has clung to a deistic belief in the existence of God. Such belief hardly amounts to Christian faith: Until the penultimate chapter of the novel, Stepan has not read the gospel for more than thirty years, and his recollection of it comes through his much more recent reading of Renan's *Vie de Jésus* (1863) (10:486–87), which treats Christ as a mortal historical figure who founded a great religion. And yet, as Stepan sits in the peasant cart on his final journey, he experiences a sense of guilt toward the peasantry, although at first he cannot precisely say in what this guilt consists (10:483). He resolves to forgive all his enemies (10:490). Suddenly he understands the meaning of the passage from the gospel according to Matthew about turning the other cheek (10:496). (The meaning has been borne in on him by Sofia Ulitina, whose first name indicates wisdom and whose patronymic, Matveevna, indicates that she is Matthew's progeny.) Thus Stepan comes at last to the central Christian truth to be developed in *The Brothers Karamazov*, particularly in the teachings of Father Zosima: All are guilty before each other (10:491). He has found "faith in the Almighty," "the only refuge of the human race amid the sorrows and trials of life" in this sinful time, that faith to which the last rites administered over him refer (10:505).

NOTES

1. That is, in the Russia of the 1870s, the doctrine that a revolutionary minority should seize political power and implement economic and social revolution "from above" irrespective of the wishes expressed by the masses.

2. See P. N. Tkachev, "Bol'nye liudi," *Izbrannye sochineniia na sotsial'no-politicheskie temy*, ed. B. P. Koz'min (Moscow: Sotsekgiz, 1932–37), vol. 3, 5–48.

3. On *pochvennichestvo*, see Wayne Dowler, *Dostoevsky, Grigor'ev, and Native Soil Conservatism* (Toronto: University of Toronto Press, 1982).

4. Dostoevsky describes the occasion in a letter of October 1867 to S. Ivanova; see 28/ii:224–25.

5. That is, a member of the urban lower middle class; Nechaev was the son of a painter.

6. On Nechaev's first sojourn abroad and on this proclamation campaign, in particular, see Philip Pomper, *Sergei Nechaev* (New Brunswick, N.J.: Rutgers University Press, 1979), 69–98.

7. Quotation from the "Catechism" in this chapter is drawn from the translation of the document in Pomper, *Sergei Nechaev*, 88–94; see, especially, 90–91 on the mentality demanded of the revolutionary.

8. As noted by the editors of Dostoevsky, *Sobranie sochinenii*, 10 vols. (Moscow: GIKhL, 1956–58), vol. 7, 756.

9. See Pomper, *Sergei Nechaev*, 25. In *The Devils*, such a system is most cogently advocated by Shigalev.

10. Ibid., 137.

11. See M. K. Lemke, *Politicheskie protsessy v Rossii 1860-kh gg.*, 2d ed. (Moscow-Petrograd: GIZ, 1923), 518.

12. It became customary for revolutionaries to follow acts of terrorism with the distribution of some leaflet explaining to the public why the act had been perpetrated.

13. The question as to the condition of the factory workers, revolutionary agitation among them, and their response to it is raised in the light of the beginnings of industrial dispute in Russia. There are echoes here of the strike by about eight hundred workers that broke out at the Neva cotton-spinning factory in St. Petersburg in May 1870, the first significant industrial dispute in Russia, which was provoked by arbitrary withholding of part of the workers' pay and which resulted in the trial of sixty-two workers in July of that year.

14. See Pomper, *Sergei Nechaev*, 94.

15. "The Posing of Revolutionary Questions"; see also Section 26 of the "Catechism of a Revolutionary," which speaks of the dashing world of the brigand, the "true and unique revolutionary in Russia" (ibid.).

16. Chernyshevsky, "Bor'ba partii vo Frantsii pri Liudovike XVIII i Karle X," *Polnoe sobranie sochinenii*, 16 vols. (Moscow: Goslitizdat, 1939–53), vol. 5, 217.

17. On Granovsky, see Leonard Schapiro, *Rationalism and Nationalism in Russian Nineteenth-Century Political Thought* (New Haven: Yale University Press, 1967), 73–81; Derek Offord, *Portraits of Early Russian Liberals: A Study of the Thought of T. N. Granovsky, V. P. Botkin, P. V. Annenkov, A. V. Druzhinin, and K. D. Kavelin* (Cambridge: Cambridge University Press, 1985), 44–78; Priscilla Reynolds Roosevelt, *Apostle of Russian Liberalism: Timofei Granovsky* (Newtonville, Mass.: Oriental Research Partners, 1986).

18. A. Stankevich, *Timofei Nikolaevich Granovskii* (Moscow: n.p., 1869).

19. See T. N. Granovsky, *Sochineniia*, 4th ed. (Moscow: Tipografiia A. I. Mamontova, 1900), 134–71.

20. Ibid., 420–37, 540–50.

21. The eighteenth-century thinker Radishchev, author of *A Journey from St. Petersburg to Moscow* (1790), is a prototype of the so-called repentant nobleman weighed down by a sense of guilt at his privileged position over his serfs.

22. Richard Peace, *Dostoyevsky: An Examination of the Major Novels* (Cambridge: Cambridge University Press, 1971), 142.

23. The revolutionary of the "Catechism" will seek to exploit "ambitious statesmen and liberals" of various descriptions, "making it appear that he is following them blindly but all the while taking them in hand, learning all their secrets, hopelessly compromising them" (see Pomper, *Sergei Nechaev*, 93).

24. On this seam, see Charles A. Moser, *Antinihilism in the Russian Novel of the 1860s* (The Hague: Mouton, 1964). Unlike many antinihilist authors, though, Dostoevsky, in *The Devils*, does not attempt a defense of the existing state and its ruling class.

25. On this seam, see Richard Freeborn, *The Russian Revolutionary Novel: Turgenev to Pasternak* (Cambridge: Cambridge University Press, 1982), chapter 1.

26. That is, the doctrine that although humans are egoists, they are also rational and may therefore be taught to understand that their own self-interest lies in performance of actions that are of benefit to others.

27. The Crystal Palace was held up by Chernyshevsky – and by Turgenev, in his novel *Smoke* (*Dym*, 1867) – as a symbol of Western achieve-

ment, but Dostoevsky turned it into a symbol of the Western peoples' concentration on the material and rational world at the expense of spiritual wholeness.

28. See Pomper, *Sergei Nechaev*, 91.

29. It is significant that one of the epithets used in the opening chapter to describe the Petrashevsky society is *protivoestestvennyi* ("against nature") (10:9).

30. It is worth noting that midwifery was the favored calling in the 1870s of young women of radical sympathies, since it involved the application of science, enabled them to play a useful, practical role in society, and gave them access to the common people for the purposes of conducting socialist propaganda.

31. Chernyshevsky, "Esteticheskie otnosheniia iskusstva k deistvitel'nosti," *Polnoe sobranie sochinenii*, vol. 2, 5–92.

32. See, especially, his article of 1861, "G-n – bov i vopros ob iskusstve" (18:70–103).

33. Dostoevsky had made a similar comparison of a real apple with one that had been painted, and with a similar polemical purpose, in an article published in 1864; see "Gospodin Shchedrin, ili raskol v nigilistakh" (20:108–9).

34. It should be noted, first, that Shigalev's "system," which ensures the death of man's spirit, is expounded at an event that masquerades as a birthday party and, second, that birthdays are not events – the narrator makes much of this point – that the Virginskys think worthy of celebration (see 10:300).

35. Chernyshevsky, "Lessing, ego vremia, ego zhizn' i deiatel'nost'," *Polnoe sobranie sochinenii*, vol. 4, 210.

36. D. I. Pisarev, "Bazarov," *Sochineniia*, 4 vols. (Moscow: Goslitizdat, 1955–56), vol. 2, 9–11.

37. "Dva lageria teoretikov" (20:6). See also the announcement inviting subscriptions to the journal *Vremia* for 1863 (ibid., 207). Dostoevsky's polemical works of the early 1860s are examined in my article "Dostoyevsky and Chernyshevsky," *The Slavonic and East European Review* 57 (1979): 509–30; see, especially, 528.

38. *Chambers 20th Century Dictionary*, ed. E. M. Kirkpatrick (Edinburgh: Chambers, 1983).

39. Subjects of German extraction came within the Russian Empire with the acquisition of Baltic provinces in the eighteenth century following Peter the Great's defeat of the Swedes in his Great Northern War (concluded

1721). Examples of noblemen of Germanic ethnic origin abound in the imperial service in nineteenth-century Russia and helped to create the impression exploited by revolutionaries such as Bakunin that the Russians, a Slav people, were oppressed by an alien state apparatus.

40. See, for example, A. P. Shchapov's pioneering work on the schism, a dissertation written at the University of Kazan' and published in 1859 under the title *Russkii Raskol Staroobriadstva* . . . ; D. L. Mordovtsev's surveys of peasant rebellions, *Gaidamachina* (1870); *Politicheskie dvizheniia russkogo naroda*, 2 vols. (1871); and S. V. Maksimov's ethnographic sketches, *Lesnaia Glush'. Kartiny narodnogo byta iz vospominanii i putevykh zametok*, 2 vols. (1871).

41. I. Pryzhov, *Istoriia kabakov v Rossii v sviazi s istoriei russkogo naroda* (1868). On Pryzhov, see Franco Venturi, *Roots of Revolution: A History of the Populist and Socialist Movements in Nineteenth-Century Russia* (London: Weidenfeld and Nicolson, 1960), 375–78.

42. That is, son of a nobleman (*barin*).

43. Dostoevsky, "Dva lageria teoretikov" (20:5).

44. In the announcement inviting subscriptions to the journal *Vremia* for 1863 (20:208).

45. See Dostoevsky's notebook for 1860–62 (20:154).

46. "Dva lageria teoretikov" (20:7).

47. She is at one point referred to as *iurodivaia* (10:133). The *iurodivyi*, or fool supposedly possessing heightened powers of insight, is a type that within the Russian religious and cultural tradition is associated with innocence and holiness.

48. Eloquence – possessed in the novel in the highest degree by Stepan Verkhovensky – is by no means a virtue in Dostoevsky's eyes: It is associated with faults (phrase-mongering, insincerity, vanity, exhibitionism) which Dostoevsky, like the radical camp, attributed to "liberals." On the other hand, lack of eloquence, although not in itself a virtue, may betoken wholesome right-mindedness in a Dostoevskian character.

49. It should be noted that, at this period, the factory workers were generally seen by Russian revolutionaries not from the Marxist perspective as an embryonic industrial proletariat quite distinct in its behavior and political consciousness from the peasantry but as a section of the peasantry itself, albeit one that sometimes proved more receptive than the rural masses to socialist propaganda.

50. Granovsky, *Sochineniia*, 472.

The Narrator
and Narrative Technique
in Dostoevsky's *The Devils*

M. V. JONES

A casual reader might be surprised to be told that the first character to appear in the opening pages of *The Devils* is Anton Lavrentevich G——v. But there is no mystery. Anton Lavrentevich is the narrator. He is unique among the narrators of Dostoevsky's four major novels in having a name, a job with career prospects (though there is no evidence as to what it is or that he spends much time at it), and, to some extent, a documented past. He is evidently a man of some intelligence, wit, education, and creative imagination (capable of writing a prose work of Dostoevskian quality, in fact). He is young[1] and unmarried, and a member of the provincial liberal intelligentsia, with a good knowledge of current affairs and an inquiring, analytical mind. He is capable of understanding the complexities of psychological conflict, political intrigue, and interpersonal relationships, but is lacking, it would seem, great spiritual depth or firm moral character. He also appears to have a prodigious, even photographic memory for the detail of past events, or possibly he is blessed with boundless inventiveness. His confidence in the liberal values of the previous generation and his curiosity about those of the young progressives have, however, been shattered by the dramatic and tragic events in which he has been involved in his town and about which he now writes. Socially, he is persona grata with the ruling classes in the province as well as being acquainted with the life of its lower ranks. He is at ease in the drawing rooms of the gentry and familiar with the hovels of the urban poor. Not only Stepan Trofimovich feels able to confide in him, but so, too, on first encounter, do such dissimilar characters as Kirillov and Liza Tushina. Before the recent events in the town that form the subject matter of his chronicle, his principal access to great events and European intellectual life was through his personal relationship with Stepan Trofimovich Verkhovensky and the little group of intellectuals he has gathered around him, most of them, however, not presentable in polite society. Stepan Trofimovich had been the nearest thing to a great national figure that the town could boast, and Anton Lavrentevich seems to have been happy to act as his confidant for nine years or more, rushing around performing errands and lending a sympathetic ear to the great man's confidences. The reader senses that he is now torn between a lingering affection and personal loyalty to his old friend and a realization that this friend was, in reality, a ridiculous, pathetic, and culpable old man from whom he now wants to distance himself. During and especially since "the events," his eyes have been gradually opened to the fact that Stepan Trofimovich's inflated image was all an illusion in which the old man and Varvara Pavlovna Stavrogina and all those who bowed down before them (a category in which he includes himself) had colluded, and that this illusion was in some way the source of the unbelief and anarchy of the next generation. Still retaining something of his respect and affection for the old man, he is nevertheless disillusioned, and an ironical note pervades his account. This irony oscillates between the affectionate and the cynical, the nostalgic and the disabused. At times it is filled with sadness; at times it tips over into angry caricature. To some degree the ironic tone is evidently a defense mechanism, for it enables Anton Lavrentevich to distance himself from his own past and draw a veil over the fact that he is now engaged in the wholesale betrayal of personal confidences. To some degree it is also irony at the expense of this past. Finally, it enables him to establish a bond with his supposed reader, also no doubt a person of education, sensibility, social standing, and worldly wisdom, unlikely to view the events in the provincial town with the same degree of absorption as a participant might feel. He has therefore to walk a tightrope, admitting that he once had close relationships with these people, while now adopting an ironic tone at their expense. The pose of journalist- chronicler suits him well.

Such is the picture the reader forms of the person telling the story. It is possible to draw a much more detailed portrait of Anton Lavrentevich, of course, observing his reactions to specific situations and individuals (for example, his falling in love with Liza Tushina, his humiliating encounter with the great writer Karmazinov, or his final vain pleadings with his mentor Stepan Trofimovich), mapping out his psychology (his tendency to see ulterior motives, his frantic desire not to be left out of unfolding events, the slightly paranoid way in which he notes the fact when he is ignored or not recognized, his indecent readiness to join the crowd of young people viewing a recent suicide, his increasingly desperate and impotent attempts to hold back the tide of catastrophe at the fête), and especially in his description of his growing estrangement from his hero as well as his fascination with Stavrogin and his intellectual emanations Kirillov, Shatov, and Peter Verkhovensky. We may suspect some rewriting of history in deference to his self-esteem, and this is important when we come to consider both the information we are given and the information withheld from us. "Rewriting" can mean adding as well as subtracting.

In fact, from the beginning, this narrator-chronicler establishes an implied contract with his readers. It seems he is committed to pass on to them only information for which he can vouch personally or for which the evidence is compelling; otherwise, he will make his reservations explicit and clear. At first sight he seems to keep to this resolve, underlining it with such comments as "Now everything is known down to the last detail about this horrible event" (10:460) or "Now that everything is over, and I am writing this chronicle, we know what it was all about, but at the time we knew nothing, and it is natural that some things seemed strange to us" (10:166).

As chronicler, he occasionally pauses to remind himself and the reader of the parameters of his own narrative: "As a chronicler, I'll limit myself to describing the events exactly, just as they happened;

I'm not to blame if they seem implausible" (10:56); or "Of course, there are now many legends circulating in our town about this period, but if anything was known for certain, it was surely limited to those who had grounds for knowing. I can only assume" (10:464); or "Of course, no one has the right to demand from me, as narrator, too detailed an account of one point: There's a secret and a woman involved" (10:360); or "There are certain things it is not my place to narrate; besides, there are some I am simply incapable of talking about. Nor is it my business to discuss administrative errors; therefore I will omit entirely the administrative side of things. In beginning this chronicle, I set myself a different set of tasks. Besides, a great deal will soon be laid bare by the Official Inquiry that has been appointed in our province" (10:267). We have to infer what that "different set of tasks" was but assume that it does not correspond with what interests the Official Inquiry.

Sometimes he draws on privileged sources: "Perhaps I shall be asked how I could have discovered such an intimate detail. Well, what if I witnessed it myself? What if, on more than one occasion, Stepan Trofimovich himself sobbed on my shoulder, depicting in vivid colors every last circumstance of the affair?" (10:12–13); or "I heard rumors from the most intimate sources (well, you may assume that Julia Mikhailovna herself . . .)" (10:337); or "He told me that himself the following day when we met briefly on the street" (10:385). On other occasions, he alludes to evidence (or lack of evidence) from unnamed sources: "In short, it's still not known for certain whether there was any outside influence or incitement" (10:335); "Therefore I am absolutely convinced. . . . There's really rather strong evidence to support this circumstance" (10:336); "I know almost for certain that . . . " (10:337); "It's pure nonsense to say that. . . . It's even greater nonsense to say that . . . " (10:336–37). Sometimes he makes a point of disputing published versions of events: "But the reports in the Moscow and Petersburg newspapers greatly exaggerated our disaster" (10:394).

Most frequently, he is his own source of validation for the events he describes, especially when they involve Stepan Trofimovich. The text is peppered with such expressions as "I saw with my own eyes how this day of shameful memory began" (10:358); "It was a very dark spot at one end of the enormous Stavrogin park. Later, I went there deliberately to have a look at the place" (10:456). At times, however, he admits, in all apparent honesty, to uncertainty and confusion about scenes in which he himself participated:

I confess that I saw nothing myself, but everyone else assured me that they had seen it, even though they couldn't possibly have seen it because of all the confusion, although some of them might have. Only I did not believe it at the time. But I remember that Nikolai Vsevolodovich looked rather pale all the way back. (10:261)

I don't recall exactly what happened next. . . . I, too, as an eyewitness, even though at some distance, was required to testify at the inquest: I declared that everything had occurred entirely by accident, through the actions of people who, while they might have been incited, were not really aware of what they were doing. They were drunk and had lost their grip on reality. I stand by that opinion even now. (10:413)

The distinguished Russian critic V. A. Tunimanov remarks that whenever the narrator is dealing with matters he witnessed himself or those of which he has heard reports, he emphasizes the relativity and uncertainty of his account (its *nedogovorennost'*, *nedoskazannost'*).[2]

His accounts often contain overt value judgments, and sometimes they have a high emotional charge. For example: "I reject with indignation the vile gossip spread around afterward" (10:379). Occasionally, they gloss an outburst that he made at the time: "To this very day I do not understand how and am amazed that I could have shouted those words at him. But I had guessed right: As it turned out later, everything occurred almost exactly as I had said" (10:384).

In some instances, the reader senses a discontinuity between what the narrator felt at the time and what he now thinks. In a valuable discussion of this issue, the American critic Gene Fitzgerald[3] suggests that we distinguish between an "experiencing self" and a "narrating self" and gives good, clear examples of the disjunction between the two. For example, in the very first chapter of the novel, Anton Lavrentevich declares that, without doubt, at one time Stepan Trofimovich was as famous as Chaadaev, Belinsky, Granovsky, Herzen, and other revolutionary thinkers, but, because of subversive activities, his career was cut short, owing to "a vortex of combined circumstances." This is the voice of the "experiencing self" (i.e., what he apparently believed at the time). Suddenly, his point of view shifts to that of the "narrating self" (what he now believes):

> And what do you think? It turned out that there had been neither "whirlwind" nor "circumstances," at least not on this occasion. Only a few days ago I learned to my great surprise, but from a most reliable source, that while Stepan Trofimovich had been living among us, in our province, not only was he not an exile, as we had been led to believe, but he was also not under police surveillance. Such is the power of the imagination. (10:8)

This disjunction, though not always overt, may be intuited throughout the text. All this enhances our sense of realism. But we also detect that underlying the narrator's stance is a more personal agenda at which, as we have seen, he himself hints. His emotional involvement with the leading character over a long period is a vital factor in this, as is his deep fascination with Stavrogin. The former is, in fact, the subject of the opening and most of the closing chapters. The latter finally closes the book. And here is his Achilles heel as a dispassionate narrator. Anton Lavrentevich needs above all to understand the spiritual and intellectual origins of the calamitous events he records and in which he participated. For he has been near or at the center of events throughout. He has been a close associate and confidant of the individual who, he now thinks, has unwittingly set all the anarchic events in train by his irresponsible and bankrupt philosophy and style of life. This closeness to events gives him privileged access to the facts but also tars him with the brush of moral and emotional collusion. After all, who else – certainly not the Commission of Inquiry – is likely to accord Stepan Trofimovich, or even Stavrogin, a central role in events, or even any role at all? We shall not be surprised, then, if he departs from his promise of objectivity at moments that matter to him personally, and it will be interesting to see which these are. I must not disguise the fact that in expressing the matter in this way, I have glossed over a number of problems widely discussed in previous academic studies.

Readers often notice that although the narrator purports to be scrupulous in revealing and assessing the reliability of much of the information he gives us, two features of his narrative seem inconsistent with this stance. The first concerns events at which he claims to have been present. His admission that he is not sure of some details of scenes that he witnessed in person is entirely true to life. But, elsewhere, his total recall of every word uttered in long and heated conversations defies all canons of realism. He would have had to have secreted a tape recorder, not yet invented, to persuade us that every detail is accurately recorded. We may decide to put this down to poetic license or the "conventions of the genre" (though what genre?). But whatever excuses we make for him, it puts seriously in question his repeated protestations of respect for evidence.

The second feature, however, is even more disquieting. There are also detailed, dramatic descriptions of private scenes at which he was not present and whose participants were either dead or far away before they could have passed on details to the narrator, even assuming that they, too, possessed total recall of events and conversations highly charged with emotion and suspense. Tunimanov, taking his cue from a passage in Dostoevsky's notebooks, calls these "*sam-drug*" (i.e., together with another person) scenes.[4] The Australian critic Slobodanka Vladiv, in her meticulous structural analysis of the novel, has listed all the "*sam-drug*" scenes, and, beginning with part 2 of the novel, there are a surprising number of them.[5] Even where the source of the narrator's information is not given, it is sometimes possible to imagine how he might subsequently have learned of those events. But the participants in other events, for example, Kirillov, Stavrogin, Shatov, Liza Tushina, and Fedka, are all dead by the time the action ends. The nearer the "*sam-drug*" scene is to the final dénouement, the more difficult it is to imagine a realistic source of information. And the narrator seems so carried away with the narrative that he entirely forgets even to mention the matter. Frequently, such scenes take on a Gothic, melodramatic coloring, suggesting that the many references to Shakespeare, as well as to Paul de Kock, George Sand, and Charles Dickens, not to mention the use of apocalyptic imagery, are not coincidental. Such are the private interviews between Stavrogin and Peter Verkhovensky, and between each of them and Kirillov and Shatov. The narrator offers no explanation for these anomalies. On one occasion he tamely ventures, after recording Peter Stepanovich Verkhovensky's thoughts: "That's what, or approximately what, Peter Stepanovich must have been thinking to himself" (10:299). On another, he comments with seemingly unwarranted confidence of Stepan Trofimovich: "That's precisely what he must have been feeling; that's precisely how he must have seen his action" (10:480). But elsewhere the narrative slips imperceptibly from chronicle into imaginative fiction. Telling us that "I can now state with certainty that there was a moment just around twilight when he was ready to get up, go out and – tell everything," the narrator even records a dream of the now dead Shatov (10:432), without offering any explanation or apology for his evident flight of fantasy.

Before offering an explanation ourselves, let us examine how others have perceived the anomaly. Tunimanov suggests that there are three basic forms of narrative in *The Devils:*

a) the tale told by the "chronicler" where the voice of the narrator is dominant; b) scenes in which the chronicler participates, where his role may vary considerably; c) intimate scenes without the participation of the chronicler where G——v disappears completely or almost completely. In addition there are the mass scenes, combining these different forms.[6]

Accepting this basic structure, Fitzgerald argues that Dostoevsky gave clear indications in his notebooks that his narrator would sometimes invent facts himself but that in all cases he can vouch for their truth: "Either I have positive facts, or I am perhaps *inventing* them myself, but in any case, I can assure you that everything is true."[7] The claim that although one is inventing facts, they are nevertheless true is neither transparently clear nor entirely convincing. Obviously "truth" here, perhaps roughly equivalent to "verisimilitude" or "conveying the spirit of the truth," is not that publicly verifiable truth on which the narrator is normally so insistent. Fitzgerald's solution is that Dostoevsky in fact "presents a plausible witness-narrator who is also an authorial figure in his own right,"[8] and that he "invents isolated conversations and scenes, but not as an extraordinary and occasional occurrence but rather as a 'realistic' aspect of his total authorial control of the work."[9] He regrets that in his fine descriptive article Tunimanov notes the fact but fails to develop it further. In other words, the narrator only does what all "objective" narrators tend to do, use his imagination to fill up gaps in the evidence and to give his narrative meaning, shape, and readability.[10] And, the argument continues, he is rather good at it, maintaining suspense, incorporating melodramatic physical detail, reproducing tense dialogue, hinting at apocalyptic overtones, and so on. Fitzgerald might have added that the extensive use of the imagination in the guise of factual reporting was not unique to Dostoevsky's narrator in *The Devils*. Dostoevsky's contemporary, the novelist N. S. Leskov, is notorious for such practices.

However, Fitzgerald effectively demonstrates that the chronicler's authorial hand is evident throughout the novel, not just in those sections where he indulges in wholesale invention. We have already noted his realistically implausible total recall of dialogues at which he was actually present. To this Fitzgerald adds graphic details of physical description in scenes from which the narrator was absent, which he transfers, Fitzgerald speculates, from scenes he witnessed.[11]

The strength of Fitzgerald's argument is that he can demonstrate that even in those scenes where the narrator is most insistent on the quality of his evidence, he deploys the traditional techniques of the novelist, both in re-creating dialogue that is beyond the scope of memory and in his mastery of narrative techniques for retaining the reader's interest. According to this reading, authorial control of the narrative is the narrator's primary requirement and this involves motivating characters and events for which direct evidence is unavailable. But why, then, does the narrator constantly insist that the primary criterion for inclusion is the quality of the evidence, even at times, with disarming candor, emphasizing its inadequacy? And why at crucial moments, when hard evidence is badly needed and in short supply, does he furtively abandon this criterion? Or to address the question on a different level to which we shall return in due course, why does Dostoevsky put him in this position?

The weakness of Fitzgerald's argument is that there is a difference between artistically embellishing or re-creating scenes of which one has firsthand or reported knowledge and the wholesale invention of scenes for which hard evidence is totally wanting, even perhaps that they took place at all. Even if we regard the appeal to hard evidence simply as a narrative device used to serve the reality principle and to engage in mystification, the anomaly remains. Only in that case we have to address our complaints to Fedor Mikhailovich Dostoevsky rather than to Anton Lavrentevich G——v.

In fact, I believe it is possible to reconcile these two positions, and that the key is to be found in the psychology of the narrator, to which allusion was made earlier. It appears that Anton Lavrentevich has not one but two agendas. One is to provide an accurate record of public events from an insider's point of view, and thereby to try to present as dispassionately as possible the subtle human factors underlying the formal and superficial factual report that the Official Inquiry is likely to produce. For this purpose, his addressee is the curious reader who needs to be reassured of the reliability of his information. The second is a personal one: to try to understand why and how his whole intellectual, spiritual, and social world has collapsed around him, sweeping away his friends and acquaintances, his social superiors, and people who have trusted him with their confidences, with one of whom (Liza) he has even briefly been in love, leaving the stage littered with the corpses of people whose company he has regularly kept and whose personalities and views have fascinated him, and to try to reorientate himself amid the wreckage. Such an agenda involves not only accurate recording and weighing of evidence; it involves getting inside the minds of the chief actors in the drama and making sense of the whole sequence of events, including his part in them. For this purpose his addressee is himself, less interested in facts than in explanatory theses. The former leads to his distancing himself emotionally from incidents in which he participated and adopting his characteristic tone of irony, though occasionally recollected emotion breaks through to the surface and leaves its trace on his rhetoric. The latter leads to his imaginative re-creation of individuals and scenes with which he is obsessed and which he finds hard to understand. In the "*sam-drug*" scenes, the narrator's ironic tone entirely disappears and dialogue is accompanied by what Vladiv calls stage directions.[12] The former agenda limits him to his chronicle, of whose rules and limitations he constantly reminds himself and the reader. The latter agenda requires frequent recourse to the conventions of the novel to probe and shape experience and to discover meaning.

Put another way, there are not one but two "narrating selves" organizing the material generated by the "experiencing self," and they derive from two different agendas. The disjunction that readers often notice, and that disturbs many,[13] seems to be grounded in the psychology of the narrator. Perhaps there are two "experiencing selves" as well, the one attending with growing anxiety to public events around him, the other wrestling with the chief actors' anguished private philosophies of life, some of which he knows by heart (that of Stepan Trofimovich), most of which he has to reconstruct in his imagination (those of Stavrogin, Kirillov, Shatov, even Peter Verkhovensky), all of which he understands with difficulty. And this imaginative wrestling is as much a part of what he has experienced as are the public events.

Was this Dostoevsky's intention in creating Anton Lavrentevich G——v and his particular mode of narrative? Although we do not have Dostoevsky's explicit confirmation,[14] it is at least not inconsistent with what we do know. It is clear why, basing his plot on the Nechaev affair, Dostoevsky needed to motivate Peter Verkhovensky, and it is not difficult to understand his choosing to incorporate a variation on Turgenev's "fathers and sons" theme according to which the nihilists of the 1860s descend from the liberals of the 1840s. It is even understandable that he chose to introduce Stavrogin as an intellectual intermediary. Moreover, Shatov, too, is necessary to the plot. But his Slavophile philosophy is not. And Kirillov seems entirely superfluous, whether as a contributor to the plot or to the philosophical dialogue. One may wonder why Dostoevsky put his narrator in a position of having to understand Shatov and Kirillov at all. The answer to these questions has to be sought in Dostoevsky's own developing plans for a novel about a "Great Sinner," partly deferred in order to concentrate on the pamphlet-novel about the Nechaev affair. There is, however, a residue of the Great Sinner project, attenuated in the person of Stavrogin but projected in caricature form in the persons and philosophies of Shatov, Kirillov, and Peter Verkhovensky, who represent three distortions of earlier stages in Stavrogin's now bankrupt philosophy of life. It has to be said that Dostoevsky found a very effective way of both exploiting and reserving his work on the Great Sinner by making use of a chronicler who lacks the insight fully to understand Stavrogin but who gets quite close to understanding the fragments of his philosophizing embodied in his disciples.

There were many advantages in choosing this type of narrator, some of them polemical and some artistic. From a polemical point of view, Dostoevsky was able, at least in principle, to distance himself from the cruder caricatures the novel contains by attributing them to a narrator with a more limited perspective than his own. From an artistic point of view, he was able to combine the techniques and advantages of both chronicler and novelist. Sometimes he used the pretext of the chronicler's perspective (telling the story in chronological order) to serve the novelist's purpose (creating suspense and mystification by withholding information). The most striking example is the buildup to the first personal appearance of Stavrogin, who appears for the first time toward the end of the first part of Dostoevsky's three-part novel, in the chapter entitled "The Wise Serpent." This is delayed even further by the unexpected arrival of Peter Stepanovich, who also appears now for the first time. Of course, by insisting on telling everything in its correct temporal sequence, the narrator defers much that he already knows, thus holding us constantly in suspense and reliving with us, as it were, the events as they happened. For example, he does not tell us whether Shatov is actually murdered until it actually happens, though he evidently knows it before he first sets pen to paper. In other words, he sacrifices the view from the top of the Eiffel Tower for the experience of wandering through the Paris streets. And even when he reaches the top, not everything appears neatly where he might have expected it to be.[15]

Another device that combines the two types of narrative is the use of the chronicler's ignorance or failure to understand to account for vital gaps in the information. In *The Idiot*, Dostoevsky had discovered, perhaps by accident, the enormous power that could be exercised over the narrative by what might be called "dynamic silence." In that Petersburg novel, possibly the most important events, in which the main characters' relationships and the eventual outcome are irrevocably determined, take place offstage, in Moscow, between parts 1 and 2. At this point in his narrative, the narrator pleads ignorance of all but the most sketchy knowledge of what went on. Similarly, in *The Devils*, Stavrogin's past and his previous philosophy of life are disclosed mysteriously and sketchily (even if we include the chapter "At Tikhon's" containing Stavrogin's confession, which Dostoevsky failed to restore when the opportunity arose). Here, though, this must be seen not simply as ignorance (for Anton Lavrentevich is quite capable of making up scenes when he feels he needs to) but also of lack of understanding. As in *The Idiot*, readers are called on to intuit the nature and force of key events. We may speculate that by placing a mystery at the center of his narrative, Dostoevsky insured himself both against wasting a valuable resource (the type of the "Great Sinner") on a pamphlet-novel, and also against losing his readers' interest by making its core too accessible. In 1876 he was to write to Vs. S. Solovev: "If the best-known wits, Voltaire for example, had, instead of using allusions, hints, innuendoes, and elisions, suddenly decided to declare everything . . . you can take it from me that they would not have had a tenth of the effect" (29/ii:102).

But when all is said and done, the narrator with limited vision was a superb way of motivating this reticence and turning it to positive use. The vacuum at the center of the novel reflects the spiritual void in Anton Lavrentevich's soul. This does not prevent him obsessively seeking what he lacks and examining other people's spiritual states. It is not clear that the narrator ever understands Stavrogin, though he gives us enough information for us to create our own picture. He frequently indicates bewilderment or uncertainty. But does he understand Kirillov, Shatov, and Peter Verkhovensky? Although Shatov's and Kirillov's philosophies are presented in some detail through various conversations, these characters are obsessed by ideas that make their broader worldviews look like caricatures. But although the narrator stresses their social awkwardness and their melodramatic histories, he does not openly mock their philosophical views. Their tragic implications are too serious, and he takes them very seriously.

He perhaps sees glimmers of "truth" in Shatov and Kirillov; with Stepan Trofimovich toward the end, he almost reaches enlightenment. But that conclusion brings the narrative full circle, for Stepan Trofimovich's was, after all, the inadequate philosophy that apparently bred the next generation of nihilists and terrorists who have wreaked such havoc, and it is therefore fitting perhaps that the concluding chapter is devoted not to Stepan Trofimovich's spiritual resurrection, but to Stavrogin's suicide. Anton Lavrentevich has progressed in his philosophical and religious understanding but hardly at all, it would seem, in spiritual enlightenment.

What Anton Lavrentevich does understand very well are the ways that people build up elaborate illusions about one another and about life and convince one another of their truth. Moreover, he understands how vulnerable this makes them to enemies who understand the mechanisms at work. This theme is first developed in the initial narrative of the relationship between Stepan Trofimovich and Varvara Pavlovna, especially in their deflating experiences of rejection among the young progressives in St. Petersburg, and in two memorable scenes in which Varvara Pavlovna declares she will never forgive her companion, one scene relating to his reaction to news of the Emancipation (10:17) and the other to his suspicions that she is expecting him to propose to her (10:18). Similar trivial incidents in which Stavrogin offends local dignitaries also display this mechanism. It is then developed in broader and broader settings, notably in the scandalous gathering at Varvara Pavlovna's house in the section entitled "The Wise Serpent" (10:127–66), in which the unveiling of Stavrogin's horrendous secret is threatened in the presence of his mother and a motley gathering, and most memorably of all in the major public scandal focusing on the *prazdnik*. The setting (or "chronotope," as Bakhtin would call it) of the scandal scene thus broadens out from the intimate dining room or drawing room scene, to that of the drawing room invaded by the vulgar public, to the grand, apocalyptic, carnival scenes that mark the final subversion of public decorum. All these scenes bear the unmistakable seal of the Dostoevskian *skandal*. These mechanisms are understood very well by Anton Lavrentevich, and he also understands that they underlie Peter Verkhovensky's revolutionary tactics, although he tends to be reductive when it comes to Peter and his gang.

The "*sam-drug*" scenes are interwoven with these scandal scenes and invariably involve the perambulations of a visitor (the narrator himself, Stavrogin, or Peter Verkhovensky) to the hovels where Shatov and Kirillov live. The "chronotope" of the road may seem at first not to be highly developed in the novel, but it begins to come into its own in Stavrogin's night walk and his encounter with Fedka; in the memorable scene in which Peter Verkhovensky humiliates himself in chasing after his idol; and, most notably, in Stepan Trofimovich's final journey, anticipating that of the great Tolstoy.

All these features of the narrative, and many more, may be attributed to the narrator's mastery of the craft of storytelling as much as to his faithfulness to the "facts." But it will be observed that, with the exception of an earlier brief discussion, I have been writing as though Anton Lavrentevich G——v, and not Fedor Mikhailovich Dostoevsky, were really the author of the novel. In fact, few casual readers make this distinction, certainly not those contemporaries who condemned Dostoevsky for his caricature of the progressive movement. To understand the narrative structure of the novel properly, however, it is essential to distinguish between the "real author" and the "fictional narrator." Here, it is fairly easy to do so by simply editing Dostoevsky out for the purposes of analyzing the text. To illustrate the difference it makes, we may reflect that whereas many of the apocalyptic allusions noted in the introduction to the present volume may be attributed either to the "real author" (if we are studying Dostoevsky's creative work) or to the "fictional narrator" (if we adhere to the contract established between us and the narrator), this is not the case with those surnames that derive from the names of birds. While the real author (Dostoevsky) may have introduced them to heighten the apocalyptic atmosphere, we have to assume that the fictional narrator uses them because he is reporting the characters' actual names. We must also distinguish both "real author," and "fictional narrator" from the "implied author." By "implied author," we mean the organizing consciousness that we intuit when we read the novel and that we unreflectively attribute to Dostoevsky, although what we intuit may go far beyond or fall far short of what the real author actually had in mind and will frequently go beyond what the fictional narrator understands. In *The Devils*, the voice of the implied author incorporates the whole narrative irrespective of whether the narrator witnessed it, heard it from reliable sources, or may be assumed to have made it up. Moreover, it also incorporates the picture the narrator unwittingly gives of himself and that affects the way we respond to his narrative.

All this might seem academic were it not for the fact that from his very earliest fiction, but particularly in his mature work, Dostoevsky continues to experiment with narrative point of view. In *The Idiot* (1868) he had switched, in ways that defy a commonsense explanation such as the one we have ventured here, from the point of view of omniscient narrator, to chronicler with limited vision, to novelist discussing with his readers the problem of writing novels.[16] In *A Raw Youth* (1875) he reverted to first-person narrative. But here, not only does the narrator have a personality of his own but, arguably, the whole novel is really a *Bildungsroman* about him and his transition through adolescence. The narrator of *The Brothers Karamazov* is more like that of *The Devils*, presenting us with similar problems of interpretation; but he has no name and his personality, though certain basic attitudes are evident, is relatively lightly sketched and he plays no role in the plot. A discussion of Dostoevsky's reasons for these shifts, both within and between novels, and how we should make sense of them, would far exceed the limits of this essay.[17] What we can say is that the shifts constantly remind us of the conventionality of narrative and of the blurred edges between fact and fiction and between facts as purveyed from different points of view. We can also say that, especially where Dostoevsky's narrator is given a distinct individual character, it emphasizes what Bakhtin has called the polyphony of the Dostoevskian text, according to which the voice of the narrator is but one voice in a chorus and the author restrains his impulse to impose a canonical reading.[18] This, too, is, of course, controversial, for the intended message of Dostoevsky's anti-nihilist pamphlet-novel is surely unmistakable. The essential point, however, is not that the author's voice is inaudible but that it is heard through a chorus in which a personalized narrator is both soloist and conductor. This we have seen to be true.

NOTES

1. Probably in his late twenties or early thirties in view of the length of time he has been part of Stepan Trofimovich Verkhovensky's retinue.

2. V. A. Tunimanov, "Rasskazchik v 'Besakh' Dostoevskogo," in *Issledovaniia po poetike i stilistike*, ed. V. V. Vinogradov et al. (Leningrad: Nauka, 1972), 125.

3. Gene Fitzgerald, "Anton Lavrent'evic G——v: The Narrator as Re-

creator in Dostoevskij's *The Possessed,*" in *New Perspectives on Nineteenth-Century Russian Prose,* ed. G. J. Gutsche and L. G. Leighton (Columbus, Ohio: Slavica, 1982), 124–26.

4. Tunimanov, "Rasskazchik v 'Besakh' Dostoevskogo," 135.

5. Slobodanka B. Vladiv, *Narrative Principles in Dostoevskij's Besy, a Structural Analysis* (Berne: Peter Lang, 1979), 170–72. See Dostoevsky's notebooks for *The Devils,* 11:92.

6. Tunimanov, "Rasskazchik v 'Besakh' Dostoevskogo," 135–36. The view that the narrative structure is a mixed type, part first-person narrative by a chronicler and third-person narrative by an omniscient narrator, is shared by Wolf Schmid, *Der Textaufbau in den Erzählungen Dostoevskijs* (Munich: Wilhelm Fink, 1973), 81–82; and Horst-Jürgen Gerigk, *Versuch über Dostojevskijs Jüngling* (Munich: Wilhelm Fink, 1965), 37. It is disputed, however, by Slobodanka Vladiv (*Narrative Principles,* 164) on grounds that are too complex to discuss here but that command serious attention. The interested reader will discover that drawing on Schmid's concept of "text interference," Vladiv concludes that the ultimate key to the structure of *The Devils* is to be found in the category of the "implied author" (*Narrative Principles,* 79–80). Her argument is ingenious but does not alter the fact that she does not locate it on the level of fictional narrator.

7. 11:92. This passage is reminiscent of Dostoevsky's letter to Katkov in which he admits of Nechaev/Verkhovensky that "my fantasy departs in very great measure from what actually occurred. . . . But it seems to me that in my inflamed mind, imagination has created the very figure, the very type, that corresponds to such a crime" (29/i:141). The difference is that Dostoevsky the novelist makes no accompanying claim to be an objective recorder of events.

8. Fitzgerald, "Narrator as Re-creator," 122.

9. Ibid., 124.

10. Tolstoy repeatedly does this in his account of historical events in *War and Peace.* Closer to home, Leonid Grossman evidently invents missing details in his biography, *Dostoevsky,* trans. Mary Mackler (London: Allen Lane, 1964). "Faction" in different forms (i.e., a conscious and intentional amalgam of fact and fiction) runs from ancient mythology to modern journalism. I am also reminded of Nora Lavrin's technique for filling the lacunae in D. H. Lawrence's biography. Being a professional illustrator, she would

begin by drawing a picture of the missing scene and use it as a stimulus for imagining his motivation for subsequent acts.

11. Fitzgerald, "Narrator as Re-creator," 127–28.

12. Vladiv, *Narrative Principles*, 166.

13. Fitzgerald ("Narrator as Re-creator," 131) gently takes me to task in reminding me that in an earlier analysis I took a rather stronger line myself: "This confusion of perspectives cannot help but undermine further the stability of the novel's structure. By undermining the unity of point of view, Dostoevsky is threatening the ultimate foundation of narrative" (Malcolm V. Jones, *Dostoyevsky, the Novel of Discord* [London: Paul Elek, 1976], 147). Although I have modified my view in the light of Fitzgerald's work, I still believe that this is true and not inconsistent with the view I set forth here. But that is the subject of another essay.

14. Vladiv (*Narrative Principles*, 41–54) sets forth and discusses the relevant passages from Dostoevsky's notebooks.

15. I have borrowed this metaphor from Roland Barthes, *La Tour Eiffel* (Paris: Delpire, 1964).

16. See Robin Feuer Miller, *Dostoevsky and 'The Idiot,' Author, Narrator, and Reader* (Cambridge, Mass.: Harvard University Press), 1981.

17. The works of Schmid and Gerigk (see note 6, above) are available to German readers. There are discussions in English of individual novels. On *The Brothers Karamazov*, see, for example, Victor Terras, *A Karamazov Companion* (Madison: University of Wisconsin Press, 1981), 84–120.

18. This is my paraphrase of Bakhtin. The reader may consult Bakhtin's own book, M. M. Bakhtin, *Problemy poetiki Dostoevskogo* (Moscow: Sovetskii pisatel', 1963), translated by Caryl Emerson as *Problems of Dostoevsky's Poetics* (Manchester: Manchester University Press, 1984).

Dostoevsky's *The Devils:*
The Role of
Stepan Trofimovich Verkhovensky

R. M. DAVISON

Discussion of this subject might seem to be unnecessary since Dostoevsky himself tells us in his notebooks why Stepan Trofimovich is in the novel: to bring about a meeting between the two generations of Westernizers, "the pure ones and the nihilists."[1] This may well be true, but we can still usefully examine the way that Dostoevsky uses Stepan Trofimovich, and certain aspects of his character deserve scrutiny. Before he had decided to "redeem" Stepan Trofimovich at the end of the novel and intended simply that he should expire of gastric catarrh, Dostoevsky feared that character's significance might be overlooked: "I want to make it plain that there was a lot more substance to that man than the comical nature of the denouement might suggest."[2] He also wrote, rather confusingly, that Stepan Trofimovich was "secondary" but "the cornerstone";[3] the confusion can be reduced if we judge that Stepan Trofimovich's personal ideological contribution puts him in most respects in the second rank of characters, whereas his circle is *both ideologically and structurally the source of the public events that follow.*[4]

In arguing that our interest in the novel flags only when Stepan Trofimovich is off the stage, Carr[5] and Simmons[6] go too far, but at least they do not underrate him. It is easy to underrate him because frequently he is presented through the gossiping and malicious narrator who may count himself as Stepan Trofimovich's friend but is not notably sympathetic to him. On other occasions, the image comes to us through the distorting vision of Mrs Stavrogin whose sense of proportion is, to say the least, unusual: When, for instance, she announces that Stepan Trofimovich is a man of "low habits"

(10:56) she is probably agitated and outraged by nothing more reprehensible than his tendency to splutter when he talks. However, it is impossible to overlook that it is Stepan Trofimovich who unmasks the generation of the sons – a central proposition of the novel – and "two negative ideas. . . . place him firmly at the center of the novel as the author's mouthpiece":[7] These ideas concern the Gadarene swine and the angel of Laodicea. On the positive side Howe has noted that it is Stepan Trofimovich "who is allowed the most honorable and heroic end."[8]

We must also consider Freeborn's argument that Dostoevsky "*always* has problems with the heroes of his novels"[9] who suffer from a variety of disabilities, including loss of centrality. The effectiveness with which Dostoevsky establishes Stavrogin's centrality in this novel is open to serious questioning and, by virtue of Stavrogin's weakness in this respect, our attention is diverted to other, more active and perhaps more complex characters such as Stepan Trofimovich.

As the notes for the novel evolved, Stavrogin emerged to oust Peter Stepanovich Verkhovensky as the hero. No such change is apparent in the case of Stepan Trofimovich who is uniformly conceived, except for the question of his redemption, throughout the notes. As Bazanov says: "In the long creative history of *The Devils*, Stepan Trofimovich Verkhovensky undergoes no notable evolution."[10] The chapter "The Final Journey of Stepan Trofimovich" was subjected to quite extensive alterations, but this is scarcely surprising: Dostoevsky was uncertain whether he would be allowed to publish "Stavrogin's Confession" and could not precisely determine the content of subsequent sections until he knew how he stood on this issue; in addition, he chose to incorporate the episode of Stepan Trofimovich's redemption, which was barely adumbrated in the notebooks. There are indications in the notebooks that Stepan Trofimovich does go off on his final wanderings after the fête, but there is no firm indication of his redemption. Even in the novel the issue is not absolutely clear, but we should not fall into the error of Wasiolek,[11] who is inclined to pay less attention to the episode in the novel largely on the grounds that it does not appear in the notebooks: The novel introduces a new element, the importance of which is in no way reduced by its absence from earlier plans.

It should be noted, however, that although Dostoevsky's conception of Stepan Trofimovich changed little, it was a stable conception of a developing and changing character (even if we exclude the change wrought by the redemption). In this respect, Stepan Trofimovich is unusual. There are changes in circumstances surrounding other characters (Shatov, for instance) or characters try to change themselves (to no useful effect in the cases of Stavrogin and Kirillov), but it is remarkable, in so hectic and eventful a narrative, that there is little psychological development of the characters: They are generally presented in finished form and remain static. The very centrality of the hero creates problems even for him: He is so precisely at the core of the novel that everything whirls around him, but he himself does not move or develop.

Stepan Trofimovich, on the other hand, develops in a way that is painful for him and illuminating for us. Dostoevsky writes: "The essence of Stepan Trofimovich lies in the fact that, though ready at first to compromise with the new ideas, he breaks with them in the end, and indignantly so (goes off with his knapsack) and *alone* refuses to succumb to these new ideas" (12:176). There is, then, more strength in Stepan Trofimovich than we might think: Inasmuch as he stands his ground when the ideological center of the novel moves to Peter Stepanovich, he is able to resist the force of circumstances; and he is able to offer a positive ideological contribution of his own as we shall see later. This striking and important development is described by Peace as "the movement away from the comic towards the serious and the positive": He argues that Stepan Trofimovich "sets out as the butt of Dostoevsky's satire and ends up as the bearer of his message."[12] Howe chronicles Stepan Trofimovich's development in a catalogue of his mutations: "The liberal as dependent, the liberal as infant, the liberal as fool (in both senses), the liberal as dandy, the liberal who tries to assert his independence, the liberal as spoiled darling of the radicals, as *agent provocateur*, as provincial, as bohemian, as bootlicker of authority, and the liberal as philosopher."[13]

There is no other character who shows so much development and variety within the timespan of the novel; nor, with the possible exception of Shatov, is there any character who so clearly increases his share of the author's sympathy as the novel progresses.

It would be misleading, however, to think of Stepan Trofimovich merely as a moving, changing background against which the other characters stand in fixed psychological and ideological postures. He is an instigator, a cause of the events in the novel (in one sense or another he is the father of both Stavrogin and Peter Stepanovich), but, more important, he also plays a significant static part in the construction of the novel: whether we agree with Mochulsky that the main action of the novel is Stavrogin's spiritual tragedy, he is indisputably correct in asserting that this tragedy is set "into the framework of Stepan Trofimovich's story."[14] It is in the most obvious sense that Stepan Trofimovich is a framework: He is a major focus of attention at the beginning of the novel and at the end. Raskolnikov, Myshkin, and the Karamazovs make early appearances in their novels, but most of the major characters in *The Devils* are kept offstage for a considerable time, partly with the purpose of building up tension for Stavrogin's eventual entrance but with the subsidiary effect of turning our interest to Stepan Trofimovich. The other respect in which he encloses the novel at beginning and end is in his relationship to the enigmatic title and epigraph of the book, which, naturally enough, appear at the beginning; but they are not explained until the end, and it is Stepan Trofimovich who finally removes the mystery from the enigma by interpreting the story of the Gadarene swine.

If the general function of Stepan Trofimovich in the novel is fairly clear, his relationship to the supposed hero, Stavrogin, is much less so. It is generally considered helpful for an understanding of the construction of *The Devils* to regard the major characters as "doubles" of Stavrogin, but Stepan Trofimovich is not usually included in this scheme of things.[15] The issue is confused by the relationship of both Stavrogin and Stepan Trofimovich to the theme of the conflict between radicals and liberals, between the sons and the fathers, and by their relationship to each other within this theme. There is an uncomfortable "dislocation of chronological strata"[16] involved in having a spiritual son (Stavrogin) who is the same age as his "father" (Stepan Trofimovich) precisely in the particular spiritual, intellectual sense that he is his "father's" son; for Stavrogin's mysteriously romantic Byronism and his Pechorinism are an approximate coeval in intellectual history of Stepan Trofimovich's forties liberalism.

This dislocation of chronology can usefully be interpreted as one of a number of indications that there is an affinity or even identity between the two characters. It is undeniable that Stepan Trofimovich has a tutor/parent role to play for Stavrogin and that he was responsible for his "whole intellectual development" (10:10). On the other hand, though he may not have noticed it himself, Stepan Trofimovich became like a son to Mrs. Stavrogin, Nikolai's mother.[17] If Stepan Trofimovich is the son of Mrs. Stavrogin, then he is not the parent/tutor of Nikolai but his brother. Dostoevsky is at pains to play down the tutor element in the relationship: "It somehow turned out quite naturally that there was not the slightest distance apparent between them" (10:35). The degree of peculiar kinship between the two is advanced even further when it is proposed that Stepan Trofimovich should marry Dasha to cover Stavrogin's sins and thus, in some sense, become the father of his son's child, which almost means that he would actually become Stavrogin. Mochulsky argues that Stepan Trofimovich's wanderings on the highroads are "the tragedy of the uprooted romantic";[18] this is entirely acceptable, but the description "uprooted romantic" sits at least as easily on the enigmatic man of iron will who hangs himself as a citizen of the canton of Uri: The epitome of *Heimatlosigkeit* for Dostoevsky was surely to die as a national of Switzerland, a nation without nationality, a state for the stateless, and a home for the homeless. Peace has considerably strengthened the argument for identifying the two characters by showing that Dostoevsky has meticulously constructed his narrative in such a way that, precisely when Stavrogin is metaphorically coming to the end of the road after his night with Liza, Stepan Trofimovich is literally starting out at the beginning of the road on his final wandering. The narrative of the two journeys is split between two people, but its essential continuity draws them close together.[19] Their closeness, in general, is indicated by a small textological point: When Dostoevsky knew that it was not going to be possible to publish "Stavrogin's Confession" in the serial version, he transferred the section about the angel of Laodicea from the "Confession" to "The Final Journey of Stepan Trofimovich." The uncertainty about the identity of the person to whom the words of the biblical quotation apply is reflected in Chirkov's observation that Stepan Trofimovich "on the threshold of death looks back over his whole life and sees these words as referring to himself. But in a much greater degree these words refer to the central figure of the novel [Stavrogin]."[20] The conclusion must be that Stepan Trofimovich is a double of Stavrogin and that the theme of the older man as the father of two spiritually wayward sons is less important in terms of literary construction than the theme of Stavrogin as a nebulous central character who is represented on the good side by Stepan Trofimovich and on the bad side by Peter Stepanovich. Obviously, there are similarities here to Raskolnikov flanked by Sonia and Svidrigailov, and to Dmitrii Karamazov flanked by Ivan and Alesha.

As a representative of the good, Stepan Trofimovich has affinities with other "good" characters in Dostoevsky. By the end of the novel, he is converted to a worldview which is similar to that of Myshkin and Zosima. He also embodies some of the ideas of Shatov, whose nationalistic faith and approximations to Christianity clearly engaged Dostoevsky's sympathy.[21] Wasiolek observes that, in the notebooks Stepan Trofimovich "is always the fool and never the hero":[22] the use of the word *fool* clearly points to Myshkin.

We have already seen that Stepan Trofimovich has a psychological function as a developing character and a structural function as a framework for the novel. As the bearer of a positive religious message, he also has an ideological function. Mochulsky does not consider Stepan Trofimovich in this context and argues that the burden of the good is carried by Shatov, Kirillov, and Tikhon.[23] But these characters are in various ways less effective than Stepan Trofimovich:

Shatov is passive, Stavrogin is static, Kirillov is manifestly mad, and Tikhon, by Dostoevsky's choice, is not even there. This last point leads Mochulsky to conclude that the omission of "Stavrogin's Confession," with its portrait of Tikhon, removed the good side of the diptych "and only the dark panel . . . remained."[24] Gibson, however, supports the present argument and claims that if the contentious chapter is omitted, then: "It is left to some stray remarks by Shatov and the narrator and, by a sublime inspiration, to the insight of the dying Stepan Trofimovich to develop the theme on the positive side."[25] Much critical attention has been devoted to the reasons that led Dostoevsky to omit this chapter, but less regard has been paid to the effect of the omission, which is that, in the absence of Tikhon, more of the burden of representing the good falls on Stepan Trofimovich.

Is his character fitted to carrying such a burden? In general, he is weak, unsuccessful, and pathetic; these features link him with the other good characters, Sonia and Myshkin, though less so with Zosima. He has, however, more specific qualifications. The final journey in search of truth, and anything else that may occur to his fevered mind, emphasizes the similarity between Stepan Trofimovich and Don Quixote. He also entertains the highflown and altogether improbable notion that his relationship to Mrs. Stavrogin is that of a knight to his lady. Chirkov observes: "The character of Stepan Trofimovich is a new and original embodiment . . . of the theme and type of Don Quixote. . . . The narrator . . . constantly mocks Stepan Trofimovich as a *poseur*. But then Don Quixote is also constantly adopting poses."[26] One will recall that Dostoevsky explicitly took Don Quixote as one of the models for Myshkin,[27] his most extensive portrayal of a good character. It is also Chirkov who indicates the other specifically good characteristic of Stepan Trofimovich when he says that the most essential thing about him "is precisely the childish (in the best sense of the word)."[28] At the beginning of the chapter "Prince Harry" the narrator describes the close and friendly relationship of equals between Stepan Trofimovich and Stavrogin because the older man "was himself a child" (10:35); later in the same section the narrator says, in connection with Stepan Trofimovich's role as tutor to Dasha Shatova and Liza Tushina: "I will repeat again: It is astonishing how children became attached to him" (10:59). Since the point is made so emphatically, we need not hesitate to see similarities to Myshkin's relationship with the children in Switzerland, together with his own childlike character; and similarities to Alesha Karamazov's relationship with the group of boys.

The ideological function that this quixotic and childlike man fulfills, the burden of the good he bears, and the positive message he formulates are principally to be found in the closing sections of the novel when he runs away to find Russia. It may legitimately be objected that he has been in Russia for a considerable time. This is true, but, in his foolishly intellectual fashion, he has been *in* Russia, not *of* it; now he runs away into the countryside in the rain, kneels down and gets his knees wet, thus baptizing himself with the sacred soil.[29] This mundane discomfort is a parallel to the incident where Alesha Karamazov waters the earth with his tears, and both episodes are demonstrations of Dostoevsky's *pochvennik* beliefs.

The dramatic highpoint of Stepan Trofimovich's public activity, however, comes earlier, in the form of his speech at the fête. It might be noted that being a true man of the forties, like Turgenev's Rudin, his greatest activity is a speech. The basic idea behind his oration is that mankind cannot exist without beauty. It is not so much the undifferentiated stupidity of the younger generation that Stepan Trofimovich attacks as its specific and destructive attitude, not to morals or religion but to aesthetic values. At this stage of the novel, Mochulsky is right to say that, for Dostoevsky, "the contemporary crisis was at root a crisis of *aesthetic consciousness*."[30] Stepan Trofimovich's devotion to the Sistine Madonna, to Raphael and Shakespeare, to Pushkin (who is better than boots) are well known. What is less certain, as we attempt to analyze his ideology, is whether he ever gets beyond preferring the beautiful to boots, whether he succeeds in moving from the aesthetic to the ethical, whether there really is a change in the categories of his thought between the impassioned aestheticism of the fête and the apparent religious conversion of his final journey.

In the closing pages of the novel, the liberal, the atheistic Westernizer, is much moved by the passage from the Bible concerning the angel of the church of the Laodiceans: "I know thy works, that thou art neither cold nor hot: I would thou wert cold or hot. So then because thou art lukewarm, and neither cold nor hot, I will spue thee out of my mouth."[31] However much these words may move Stepan Trofimovich, it is doubtful that they actually take him into the realms of truly ethical convictions. The implication of the quotation from the Apocalypse is that the value of a conviction is determined by the strength with which it is held or (and this seems to be of equal value) rejected. While it may be unsound categorically to describe "heat" and "cold" as aesthetic criteria used as a test of the validity of convictions, it is at least clear that by no remotely coherent inference are they ethical criteria.

Later, there is a crucial passage where Dostoevsky, while characteristically keeping the issue undecided, does nevertheless put his finger precisely on the point at which Stepan Trofimovich may have changed. The narrator is speaking:

Whether in fact he was converted, or the majestic ceremony of the administration of the sacrament profoundly moved him and awoke the artistic sensibility of his nature, but he firmly and, I am told, with great feeling uttered some words that were in direct contradiction to many of his former convictions.

"My immortality is necessary because God would not wish to commit an injustice by extinguishing completely the flame of love for Him once it had been kindled in my heart. And what is more precious than love? Love is higher than existence, love is the crown of existence and how is it possible that existence should not be subject to it? If I have come to love Him and have rejoiced in my love, is it possible that He would extinguish me and my joy and turn us into nothing? If there is a God, then I, too, am immortal. *Voilà ma profession de foi.*"[32]

This is instructive in a number of ways. First, Dostoevsky begins with a careful ambiguity: "Whether in fact he was converted . . . " Then we once again have, even at this stage, the suggestion that Stepan Trofimovich is motivated by aesthetic considerations. Third, having tantalized us with the old aesthete, Dostoevsky spells out for us, entirely without ambiguity, that the new Stepan Trofimovich is, in some measure, in direct contradiction to the old: The *profession de foi* asserts that love is the highest value and thereby stands in refutation of the aesthetic credo delivered at the fête. If Stepan Trofimovich does move from the aesthetic to the ethical, if he is converted, then this is the point at which it happens and at which we leave the aesthetic behind us.

We still do not know for certain what has happened. Stepan Trofimovich may, with his usual flair for the Gallic and the melodramatic, be pleased to call his declaration a *profession de foi* but it can equally well be read as a cry of hope against hope, of despair. Peace writes that "the last pilgrimage of Stepan Trofimovich and the arrival of Marie Shatov . . . represent a desperate attempt to save a great idea,"[33] and in the passage under discussion we see Stepan Trofimovich still attempting to get somewhere rather than arriving there. The idea that Stepan Trofimovich might be saved by his pilgrimage, just as Shatov might be saved by the arrival of his wife and the birth of her child, suggests an affinity between these two characters that is illuminating.[34] Stavrogin is notoriously unable to elicit from Shatov a plain statement of belief in God: "I . . . I will believe in God" (10:201) may be compared with Stepan Trofimovich's questions which are perhaps not altogether rhetorical, and with his hopeful proposition "If there is a God . . ." Mrs. Stavrogin, who apparently knows about such things, promptly tells him that there is indeed a God and then instructs Stepan Trofimovich to renounce his previous follies and beliefs. Since he has ostensibly done just precisely this, the narrator is moved to observe that Mrs. Stavrogin had, it would seem, not altogether understood the *profession de foi*. It is, however, arguable that precisely the opposite is the case: Mrs. Stavrogin is a remarkably silly woman, but on this occasion her ear has caught the note of indecision which has escaped the narrator, the note of aspiration, of desperation even, rather than of achievement; and what trust, it might be asked, can be placed in a man who, at the last moment, pulls the rug from under his own feet: A statement of faith is one thing; a *profession de foi*, at least for Dostoevsky, who regarded all Frenchmen as unsatisfactory variations on a theme of Voltaire, is another.

There is a further sense in which Stepan Trofimovich is not redeemed: On his final journey, he does not reach his destination. When he sets out, he is quite determined not to have a destination and does not hire horses because he does not know where he is going (and because he does not want Mrs. Stavrogin to catch him). But as his journey progresses, it transpires that he is destined to go to Spasov (Salvation) on the other side of the lake, which is provided for the drowning of the Gadarene swine. It can scarcely be an accident that the village is so named, nor is it an accident that the wanderer stays to die on this side of the water. In his handling of the point, Dostoevsky demonstrates convincingly that he is a novelist and not a philosopher or theologian. If Stepan Trofimovich does not reach his destination, if he is not redeemed, it is not because his ontology was unsound or because of the *filioque* heresy; nor is it because he was a bad man who sent his son from Berlin by parcel post when he was a baby; it is not because, being an unbeliever, he kept an icon lamp for the sake of appearances; or because of any of the other innumerable wickednesses of his surpassingly silly life. In novelistic terms, in terms of the story, of the narrative of the novel, his failure to enter the Kingdom of Heaven is attributable to an unfortunate conjunction of gastric catarrh and the timetables of the public transport system: He was too ill to get on the boat that would have taken him to Spasov (Salvation) (10:496).

If we dismiss Sonia Marmeladova, Myshkin, and Zosima (to say nothing of Makar Dolgoruky) as inherently improbable creations, Stepan Trofimovich joins the more credible company of Shatov and Alesha Karamazov as one who gets as close to Christianity as Dostoevsky could ever manage to get himself. Peace says that Stepan Trofimovich's religion is like "some vague theism of the forties" rather than "true Christianity";[35] and Rahv supports this view in saying that Dostoevsky's religion is "little more than an anarcho-Christian version of that 'religion of humanity' by which Dostoevsky himself was inspired in his youth, when . . . he took for his guides and mentors such heretical lovers of mankind as Rousseau, Fourier, Saint-Simon, and George Sand."[36] This is probably not the right ground from which to question the validity of Stepan Trofimovich's redemption. It is reasonable to suppose, for the purpose of discussion, that we know what "true Christianity" is, but we must allow for the fact that the theism even of the Slavophiles, the most convinced believers of the forties, was scarcely satisfactory from a Western point of view and quite deliberately made no attempt to render itself respectable in terms of Western theology. Dostoevsky's own religion, in his moments of greatest conviction, was an unusual form of Christophilia rather than "true Christianity," but, in the context of the Russian intellectual (or anti-intellectual) tradition, we cannot reasonably ask for more. The sins of the fathers will be visited on the children who have compounded those sins by distorting the ideas of their fathers (as Stepan Trofimovich complains when he reads Chernyshevsky's *What Is to Be Done?*) (10:238); but for those who do not distort, for Stepan Trofimovich and Shatov, there is at least the hope and the possibility, if not the full reality, of redemption.

The very uncertainty of his redemption makes it easy to overlook Stepan Trofimovich as one of Dostoevsky's good characters. Bakhtin complains that "he lacks a 'dominating idea' to determine the core of his personality; he lacks his own truth but has only separate impersonal truths, which, by virtue of that fact, cease to be fundamentally true."[37] This may well be so, but it is a virtue, not a failing, and ensures that Stepan Trofimovich is not a walking idea but a credible, contradictory human being. His confusion and uncertainty make him more plausible and convincing: It is just possible to believe that this man would kneel down in the rain and get his trousers muddy, whereas it is rather harder to accept that Alesha Karamazov would water the earth with his tears and would then, for no obvious or convincing reason, leap to his feet greatly refreshed.

The unobtrusiveness of Stepan Trofimovich's virtue has helped many critics to discount his positive contribution to the ideology of the novel. Jones, for instance, admits that a representation of the divine, albeit distorted, debased, and travestied, is to be seen in the "pathetic posturing and preaching"[38] of Stepan Trofimovich but later asks "whether there is any answer, any source of regeneration, in the novel. The easy answer is no."[39] While this is true, is it not a particular merit of Stepan Trofimovich that he does not provide the easy answer, that he does not immediately leap to the mind as one striving officiously to be good?

Finally, the humorous element in Stepan Trofimovich's character simultaneously distracts attention from his ideological importance and contributes to his literary effectiveness. In many ways he becomes more serious as the novel progresses, but he never loses substantial elements of the ridiculous. He goes to seek salvation armed with an umbrella; at the very moment of what might be his conversion, he drops again into French; in anticipation of his great speech on aesthetics, we are told that Stepan Trofimovich regarded the occasion as "one that would decide his fate," an undoubtedly dramatic assessment that is rendered rather less so by the immediate addition of the words "or something like that" (10:371); Dostoevsky introduced into *The Idiot* a little German poet whose role in life was not to have the Chinese vase fall on him, but Stepan Trofimovich surpasses this in a tour de force of creative negativity when something does not happen to him which is exactly the same as what did not happen to someone else.[40] Dostoevsky's regard for Don Quixote shows that he was aware of the value of the comic in portraying the "good man," but nowhere in the gallery of such characters do the solemn pretensions of virtue find themselves undercut by farce so constantly and so successfully.

Stepan Trofimovich has important structural, psychological, and ideological functions to perform in this novel. He is the first and almost the last figure to be seen; he constantly engages our attention as his character develops under pressure; a double of Stavrogin on the side of the good, he is the main source of hope in the work. He has affinities with other bearers of great messages in Dostoevsky but, because of his uncertain achievement of the redemption his goodness deserves, because of the unobtrusiveness of his virtue, and because of his abiding foolishness, he is, from a literary point of view, the most successful.

NOTES

1. *PSS*, 11:68. Translations of passages from the notebooks are based, with corrections where necessary, on Fyodor Dostoevsky. *The Notebooks for the Possessed*, edited and with an introduction by Edward Wasiolek, translated by Victor Terras (Chicago: University of Chicago Press, 1968). Hereafter, Wasiolek, *Notebooks*.

2. *PSS*, 11:166. This may be a draft of a passage that is intended for the narrator of the novel.

3. Edward Wasiolek, *Dostoevsky: The Major Fiction* (Cambridge, Mass.: MIT Press, 1964), 111.

4. Ibid., 113.

5. E. H. Carr, *Dostoevsky* (London: Allen and Unwin, 1931), 220.

6. Ernest J. Simmons, *Dostoevsky* (London: Lehman, 1950), 203.

7. Richard Peace, *Dostoyevsky: An Examination of the Major Novels* (Cambridge: Cambridge University Press, 1971), 205–6.

8. Irving Howe, "Dostoevsky: The Politics of Salvation," in *Dostoevsky: A Collection of Critical Essays* (Englewood Cliffs, N.J.: Prentice-Hall, 1962), 53–70; see 69.

9. Richard Freeborn, *The Rise of the Russian Novel* (Cambridge: Cambridge University Press, 1973), 179.

10. *PSS*, 12:226. V. G. Bazanov is the editor of this volume.

11. Wasiolek, *Notebooks*, 11–13, 234.

12. Peace, *Dostoyevsky: An Examination of the Major Novels*, 201.

13. Howe, "Dostoevsky: The Politics of Salvation," 69.

14. Konstantin Mochulsky, *Dostoevsky: His Life and Work* (Princeton, N.J.: Princeton University Press, 1967), 444.

15. See, for instance, Howe, "Dostoevsky: The Politics of Salvation," 68.

16. There is a useful discussion of this issue in Peace, *Dostoyevsky: An Examination of the Major Novels*, 154–56.

17. Although it supports the present argument, Peace's citation (*Dostoyevsky: An Examination of the Major Novels*, 155) of Mrs Stavrogin's declaration after the death of Stepan Trofimovich that she has no son (10:507) pushes the point a little too far. The words "as though she had uttered a prophecy" (which Peace quotes) surely move the reader on to the "Conclusion" and the death of Nikolai, Mrs Stavrogin's real, physical son.

18. Mochulsky, *Dostoevsky: His Life and Work*, 443.

19. Peace, *Dostoyevsky: An Examination of the Major Novels*, 201 ff.

20. N. M. Chirkov, *O stile Dostoevskogo* (Moscow: Nauka, 1967), 181; *PSS*, 10:497, and 11:11.

21. Peace, *Dostoyevsky: An Examination of the Major Novels*, 165, 204, 306.

22. Wasiolek, *Notebooks*, 12.

23. Mochulsky, *Dostoevsky: His Life and Work*, 416.

24. Ibid., 466.

25. A. Boyce Gibson, *The Religion of Dostoevsky* (London: SCM, 1973), 145–46.

26. Chirkov, *O stile Dostoevskogo*, 186.

27. Mochulsky, *Dostoevsky: His Life and Work*, 345–46.

28. Chirkov, *O stile Dostoevskogo*, 187.

29. Howe, "Dostoevsky: The Politics of Salvation," 70.

30. Mochulsky, *Dostoevsky: His Life and Work*, 443.

31. Revelation, 3:15–16. This passage gives an incidental insight into the reasons for the personal antipathy between Turgenev and Dostoevsky.

32. *PSS*, 10:505. It should be noted that some published translations of this passage are unreliable and fail to reproduce the vagaries of Dostoevsky's syntax.

33. Peace, *Dostoyevsky: An Examination of the Major Novels*, 310–11.

34. Howe, "Dostoevsky: The Politics of Salvation," 70. But Howe is quite clear that both Shatov and Stepan Trofimovich are, in fact, redeemed.

35. Peace, *Dostoyevsky: An Examination of the Major Novels*, 205.

36. Quoted in Howe, "Dostoevsky: The Politics of Salvation," 57.

37. M. M. Bakhtin, *Problemy poetiki Dostoevskogo* (Moscow: Sovetskii pisatel', 1963), 128.

38. Malcolm V. Jones, *Dostoyevsky: The Novel of Discord* (London: Paul Elek, 1976), 130.

39. Ibid., 151.

40. *PSS*, 10:342–43. This is the incident with Avdot'ia Tarapygina.

III   PRIMARY SOURCES

Extracts from Dostoevsky's Correspondence Relating to *The Devils*

TO A. N. MAIKOV, 12 (24)[1] FEBRUARY 1870,
FROM DRESDEN

After a long interval between [epileptic] fits, they have now taken to striking me again; and what really incenses me about them is that they get in the way of my work. I have set about an idea rich in possibilities – I am speaking not about how I will carry it out, but about the idea itself. It is one of those ideas that produce an undoubted effect on the public. Something like *Crime and Punishment*, but even closer, even more urgently related to reality, and touching directly on the most important contemporary issues. I shall finish it toward autumn, but I shall not go too fast and rush it. I shall try to have it in print by the autumn, but, if not, it doesn't matter. I hope it will earn me at least as much as *Crime and Punishment*, so that by the end of the year there will perhaps be some hope of my getting my affairs in order and returning to Russia. Only it's much too hot a theme. Never before have I worked with such enjoyment and ease.

TO N. N. STRAKHOV, 26 FEBRUARY (10 MARCH) 1870,
FROM DRESDEN

I shall tell you straight out that I have never invented a plot just for money, simply because I have undertaken to write something for a deadline. I have always entered into an agreement and sold my work only when I already had in my head a subject that I wanted to write about and felt the need to write about. Such is the subject I have now.

I won't go into detail about it, but I will say this: Rarely have I come up with anything more novel, more complete, and more original. I can say this without fear of being thought vain, because I am speaking here only of the subject, of the idea that has formed in my head, and not about how I shall bring it to realization. Such realization is in the hands of God; I am quite capable of making a mess of it, as has often been the case with me in the past. But something inside me says that inspiration won't desert me. But I can vouch for the novelty of the idea and the originality of the approach, and for the time being I look upon my idea with rapture . . .

And so I await your reply. Apart from all this, I have a great and most urgent favor to ask of you: if possible, send me Stankevich's little book on Granovsky.[2] I'll pay you later (the same arrangement as when you sent me *War and Peace*). Please do me this great favor, and I'll remember it forever. I need this book as I need air itself, and as quickly as possible since it is material essential for my writing, material I simply cannot do without. For the sake of Christ, don't forget to send it if at all possible.

TO N. N. STRAKHOV, 24 MARCH (5 APRIL) 1870,
FROM DRESDEN

I hasten to reply to you, dear Nikolai Nikolaevich, and first of all about matters relating to myself. I must tell you frankly and finally that, taking everything into account, there is no way I can dare promise a novel for the autumn issues. It seems to me that this is quite impossible, and I would ask the editors not to make things difficult for me in my work, which I would like to carry out thoroughly, giving it my best efforts. . . . One thing I will assure you is that I shall have it done by January of next year. This work of mine is dearer to me than everything. It is one of my most cherished ideas, and I want to make a good job of it.[3] At the moment I am engaged on a certain piece for *The Russian Herald* – I shall finish it soon. I am still *significantly obligated* to them. If, out of extreme need, I were to turn now to Katkov and tell him everything, it would clearly mean that my future work should also be assigned to him. I am trying to explain everything frankly to you. (As far as the piece I am writing for *The Russian Herald* is concerned, I have high hopes for it, but from a tendentious, rather than artistic, point of view. I want to utter certain ideas, even if my artistry perishes in the process. But I am being swept along by what my mind and heart have stored up. Even if it turns out to be merely a pamphlet, I shall nevertheless have my say. I am hopeful of success, but then whoever sits down to work without hope of success?) . . .

I shall finish my work for *The Russian Herald* soon, and shall sit down to my novel with enjoyment. I have had the idea for this novel within me for three years now, but hitherto I was afraid of starting it while abroad and wanted to wait until I was in Russia. But much has come to fruition over three years, the whole plan of the novel, and I think I could start on the first section (the one I have promised to *Dawn*) even while I am here, for the action starts many years ago. Don't be alarmed when I speak of "the first section." The whole idea demands the grand scale, something at least comparable to Tolstoy's novel in size. But this will be made up of five separate novels, separate to the extent that some of them (apart from the two middle ones) could even appear in different periodicals as completely self-contained stories, or even be published in separate editions as completely finished works. The overall title, by the way, will be *The Life of a Great Sinner*, although each section will also have its own particular title. Each section (that is, each novel) will be no more than fifteen galley pages in length.[4] I shall have to be back in Russia for the second novel. Its action will take place in a monastery, and although I am extremely familiar with Russian monastic life, I should still like to be in Russia. I would dearly like to go into more detail with you, but what can you say in a letter? Let me repeat: It's impossible for me to promise anything for this year. Don't rush me and you will get something that will be conscientious and perhaps even good. (At the very least, I have made this idea the aim of the whole of the rest of my literary career, for there is no point in reckoning on more than another six or seven years of living and writing.)

TO A. N. MAIKOV, 25 MARCH (6 APRIL) 1870, FROM DRESDEN

Most dear and kind Apollon Nikolaevich, I am guilty of taking until now to reply to you when I have been bursting to write to you every day. But first there's work, and then my health and hypochondria, which has returned as a result of my solitude. I have been extremely worried about my health. My heart rhythm is very uneven, and I cannot sleep. I went to the doctor, by the way, a renowned professor, and he gave me a good looking over: "Absolutely nothing wrong; it's only nerves, but your nerves are very overwrought." I need to get out of Dresden for the summer – to the sea would be good, to bathe. It would be good for my wife, too. Without doubt, the air of my native land would be best of all, and all you say on this matter in your letter is the absolute truth, beyond all doubt. But do you really not know, Apollon Nikolaevich, why I don't go back and why I cannot leave these accursed foreign parts? What's the point in arriving back only to go straight to debtors' prison. There's no way I can return for some time yet, but don't you think I don't long for Russia and want to return with all my soul? . . .

What you say about writing while here is right on target: I am indeed losing touch – not with the spirit of the time, not with what is going on in Russia (I am probably much better informed about this than you, for *every day*(!) I read *three* Russian newspapers from cover to cover, and I receive two journals). No, I am losing touch with the living flow of Russian life – not its spirit, but its flesh; and I know how important this is for artistic work! . . .

At the moment I am working on something for *The Russian Herald*. I am indebted to them, and, having given *The Eternal Husband* to *Dawn*, I put myself in a difficult situation with *The Russian Herald*. No matter what, I must finish what I am presently writing for them. I have made them a firm promise, and in literary matters I am an honest man. What I am writing is a tendentious thing; I want to speak out in an impassioned way. (The nihilists and Westernizers will cry out that I am a *retrograde*!) Well, let them; but I shall have my say in full . . .

I have not written anything for a whole year and a half now, and writing wearies me (I don't count *The Eternal Husband*). I am not putting all that much into what I am writing for *The Russian Herald*, but, on the other hand, I am promising something good for *Dawn*, and I want to make a good job of it. This project for *Dawn* has been maturing in my mind for two years now. It is the same idea I have already written about to you, and it will be my final novel. It will be about the size of *War and Peace*, and the idea is one you will approve, at least insofar as I can judge from our previous discussions. This novel will consist of five long tales (each fifteen galley pages long – in two years I have planned it out completely). The tales are independent from one another, so that they could be sold separately. The first tale I have promised to Kashpirev:[5] here, the action takes place in the 1840s. (The overall title of the novel will be *The Life of a Great Sinner*, but each tale will have its own title.) The main idea that will run through all the parts is one that has tormented me consciously and unconsciously all my life: the existence of God. In the course of his life the hero is first an atheist, then a believer, then a fanatic and sectarian, then an atheist again. The second tale will take place entirely in a monastery. I am placing all my hopes on this second tale. Perhaps people will finally say that not all I have written is trivial. (To you alone, Apollon Nikolaevich, I shall confess that in this second tale I want to present Tikhon Zadonsky as the main figure – under a different name, of course, but also a bishop who has retired to a monastery.)[6] The future hero of the whole novel, a thirteen-year-old boy, already mature and corrupted (I know the type), has taken part in the commission of a criminal act and has been placed in the monastery by his parents (members of our educated society) for instruction. The little wolf and child-nihilist gets to know Tikhon (well, you know Tikhon's character and personality). In the same monastery I shall place Chaadaev,[7] also under a different name, of course. Why shouldn't Chaadaev spend a year in a monastery? Imagine that after his first article, as a result of which he was placed under weekly medical supervision, Chaadaev did not stop but went on to publish a pamphlet, say, abroad and in French. It could well be that for that act he would be confined to a monastery for a year. Others could come to visit him: Belinsky, for instance, or Granovsky, or even Pushkin. (For it is not actually Chaadaev I am depicting in my novel, but the type he represents.) . . . But the main thing is Tikhon and the boy. For God's sake, don't say anything to anyone about the content of this second part. I never tell anyone about my themes in advance, I'm somehow ashamed. But to you I confess myself. It may well be that all this means nothing to others, but to me it is precious. Don't say anything about Tikhon. I wrote to Strakhov about the monastery but did not mention Tikhon. Perhaps I shall depict a majestic, *positive* holy figure. This will not be Kostanzhoglo[8] nor the German from *Oblomov* (I forget his name);[9] and it will not be one of your Lopukhins or Rakhmetovs.[10] To tell the truth, I shall not be creating anything but merely presenting the real Tikhon, someone I have long taken to my heart with rapture . . .

There is nothing to be said about nihilism. Just wait while this upper class, which has torn itself away from the Russian soil, completely rots away. You know, it strikes me that many of these very same young scoundrels, these decaying youths, will end up becoming real, firm believers in the Russian soil, pure Russians. As for the rest, well let them rot. They'll end up silent and paralyzed. But they are scoundrels all the same!

TO V. V. KASHPIREV, 15 (27) AUGUST 1870, FROM DRESDEN

As you probably know, I have been working on a novel for *The Russian Herald* since the beginning of the year. I was hoping to finish it for sure by the end of the year. I had already written fifteen galley sheets. Throughout my work on it the novel went slowly, and finally I was repelled by it. Nevertheless, I could not abandon its basic idea.

It had drawn me in. Then my fits. Resuming work after my illness some three weeks ago, I saw that I could no longer continue writing my novel, and I wanted to tear it up. For two weeks, I was in a very difficult situation, and then about ten days ago I recognized the really weak point in all I had written. Now I have decided finally to destroy everything and to rework the novel radically. And although some of what I have written will go into the new version, it will also be in a radically different form. Therefore I am obliged to start from scratch and redo the work of almost an entire year. Consequently, there is no way I can manage to have the novel for *Dawn* ready by the start of the year.

TO S. A. IVANOVA, 17 (29) AUGUST 1870,
FROM DRESDEN

The novel I have been working on was large and very original, but its idea was of a kind that was somewhat new for me, requiring a great deal of arrogance to pull it off. But I could not pull it off, and I failed. The work was going slowly. I felt that there was a major flaw in the whole thing, but what this was exactly I could not work out. In July, after my last letter to you, I fell ill with a whole series of epileptic fits (every week). They shook me up so much that I could not even think of work for a whole month, and I was in real danger. And then, on getting down to work again two weeks ago, I suddenly saw all at once where the weakness lay and where I had been going wrong, where-upon a new plan for the novel came to me all by itself, in a flash of inspiration, and fully formed. Everything needed to be radically changed. Without a moment's thought I crossed out everything I had written (fifteen sheets, more or less), and started again from the first page. The work of a whole year was written off. Oh, Sonechka, if only you knew how hard it is to be a writer and to bear this burden! Believe me, I know for a fact that if I had two or three years in which to compose this novel, like Turgenev, Goncharov, or Tolstoy have, I would write the sort of thing they would still be talking about in a hundred years' time!

TO M. N. KATKOV, 8 (20) OCTOBER 1870,
FROM DRESDEN

One of the most important incidents in my story will be the murder of Ivanov by Nechaev, which is well known in Moscow. Let me quickly make a reservation: I know neither Nechaev nor Ivanov nor the circumstances of that murder, apart from what I have read in the newspapers. And even if I had known them, I would not have tried to copy them. I only take the accomplished fact. It may well be that my fantasy departs in very great measure from what actually occurred, and my Peter Verkhovensky may be nothing like Nechaev. But it seems to me that, in my inflamed mind, imagination has created a figure, a type, who corresponds to that crime. Without doubt, to present such a type is not without value, but it alone would not have tempted me. In my view, these pitiful freaks are not worthy of literature. To my own surprise, this figure is emerging as half-comic. And therefore, despite the fact that this occurrence occupies one of the most important planes of the novel, it is nevertheless only an accessory and an adjunct to the activities of another figure who really can be described as the main character of the novel.

This other character (Nikolai Stavrogin) is also a dark figure, a villain. But to me he seems a tragic figure, even though many who read the work will say, "What is this?" I set out to write about this character because I have wanted to depict such a type for too long already. In my view this is a character that is both Russian and typical. I shall be very, very disappointed if it doesn't come off. I shall be even more disappointed if people consider him a stilted figure. I have taken him from my heart. Of course, this is a character who is rarely seen in all his typicality, but it is a Russian type (of a certain social class). But wait until the end of the novel before judging me, my dear Mikhail Nikiforovich! Something tells me that I shall succeed in pulling it off with this character. I shall not go into detail about him now. I am afraid of saying the wrong thing. I shall merely observe that I have depicted the character entirely through scenes and action, and not by means of analysis. I am hopeful that the character will turn out well.

For a long time I could not get the beginning of the novel right. I reworked it a few times. To tell the truth, something has happened with this novel that has never happened with me before: For weeks I stopped writing from the beginning and instead wrote from the end. Apart from that, I also fear that the beginning itself could be livelier. After five and a half galley pages (which I am sending) I have still hardly begun to develop the intrigue. However, the intrigue, the action, will broaden out and will unfold unexpectedly. I can vouch for the future interest of the novel. It seems to me that it will get better than it is now.

But there won't just be dark characters. There will also be luminous ones. I am always afraid that much will be beyond my powers. For example, I want to tackle for the first time a certain character type that has hardly been touched by literature. As the ideal of such a type I have taken Tikhon Zadonsky. My character is also a holy man who has retired to a monastery. I shall confront my hero with him and bring them together for a while. I am terribly afraid; I have never tried this before, but I do know a thing or two about this world.

TO A. N. MAIKOV, 9 (21) OCTOBER 1870,
FROM DRESDEN

Dear Apollon Nikolaevich, you and I are no longer children. We know for a fact, for example, that when something happens to Russia – not necessarily a calamity, but even serious disorders – then the most un-Russian element in our society – that is, the liberal, the Petersburg official, or the student – even these people become Russians and begin to feel themselves to be Russian, even though they may be ashamed to admit it. At some point during the winter I read in *The Voice* a serious claim, made in a progressive article, to the effect that "during the Crimean campaign, so they say, we rejoiced at the successes of the allied armed forces and at our own defeats." No, my liberalism never went that far. I was still in prison camp then, and I did *not* rejoice at the success of the allies. Along with my comrades, poor unfortunate wretches and soldiers, I felt myself to be a Russian and wished success to the Russian forces. And although I was still then under the strong ferment of the mangy Russian liberalism preached by turd-eaters like the dung-beetle Belinsky and his ilk, I did not consider myself as being illogical in feeling Russian. In truth, the facts have also revealed that the sickness gripping civilized Russians was much more severe than we ourselves imagined and that the matter did not end with the Belinskys, Kraevskys,[11] and the like. Rather, that which the evangelist Luke witnessed has come to pass – the devils possessed the man, and their name was legion, and they besought him that he would suffer them to enter into the swine, and he suffered them. The devils entered the herd of swine, and the whole herd ran violently down a steep place and into the sea and were all drowned. When them that lived nearby came to see what had taken place, they saw the man that was possessed, clothed, and sitting at the feet of Christ; and they also which saw it told them by what means he that was possessed of the devils was healed. Exactly the same thing has happened in Russia. The devils have departed from the Russian man and entered into the herd of swine, that is, into the Nechaevs, the Serno-Solovevichs,[12] and so on. These have drowned, or will do so for sure, and the healed man, out of whom the devils have departed, is sitting at the feet of Christ. So it had to be. Russia has puked up this filth she has been fed, and, of course, in these puked-up bastards nothing Russian remains. And mark, my dear friend, he who loses his people and his nationality loses also his faith in his fatherland and his god. Well, if you want to know, this is the theme of my novel. It is called *The Devils*, and it is a description of how these devils entered the herd of swine. No doubt I shall write it badly. Being more of a poet than an artist, I am always choosing themes that are beyond me. And, for that reason, I shall spoil it, I am sure. The theme is too powerful. But since none of those who have criticized my work up until now have refused to concede that I have some talent, then probably there will be pages even in this long novel that will not be bad. Well, there you have it.

In Petersburg, apparently you still have many *clever* people who, although they are horrified by the bastards entering the swine, nevertheless still dream of how good it was in the liberal-humanist times of Belinsky, and how it is necessary to bring back the culture of that period. Well, you can even see this idea among the most recently converted nationalists and others. The old-timers don't give up: the Pleshcheevs,[13] the Pavel Annenkovs,[14] the Turgenevs, as well as entire journals like *The Russian Herald*, all adhere to this tendency.

TO N. N. STRAKHOV, 9 (21) OCTOBER 1870,
FROM DRESDEN

Never before has anything cost me so much effort. Initially, that is, at the end of last year, I looked upon this work as something labored and contrived; I looked down on it. Then real inspiration visited me, and suddenly I came to love the work and seized it with both hands, even though it meant crossing out what I had already written. Then, in the summer, another change: Yet another character emerged with claims to be the real *hero of the novel*, so that the previous hero (a curious figure, but one unworthy of the name hero) receded to a secondary plane. The new hero so captivated me that I undertook yet another revision. And now, when I have already submitted the beginning of the first part to *The Russian Herald*, I have suddenly taken fright. I am afraid I might have bitten off more than I can chew. I am seriously, excruciatingly afraid! But, nevertheless, I have not brought in the new hero out of nowhere. I made preparatory notes for the whole of his role in the plan of the novel (my plan runs to several galley pages), and the whole role is set out only by means of scenes, that is, action, and not analysis. Therefore I think the character will come off, and perhaps will even be something *new*. I hope so, but I am afraid. It is time finally to write something serious.

TO A. N. MAIKOV, 2 (14) MARCH 1871,
FROM DRESDEN

Your flattering opinion of the beginning of my novel delighted me. Lord, how afraid I was, and still am. By the time you read this, you will probably also be reading the second half of the first part in the February issue of *The Russian Herald*. What will you have to say about it? I am afraid. I am afraid. As for the rest of it, I am simply in despair wondering whether I shall bring it off successfully. By the way, there will be four parts in all – forty galley pages. Stepan Trofimovich is a secondary character. The novel will not be about him at all, but his story is closely bound up with other (main) events in the novel, and I have therefore taken him as the cornerstone of everything, as it were. But, nevertheless, Stepan Trofimovich will have his moment in the fourth part, where there will be an extremely original resolution of his fate. I won't be answerable for all the rest, but for that passage I am prepared to answer in advance. But again I tell you: I am as fearful as a frightened mouse. The idea seduced me, and I have come to love it terribly, but will I handle it well or am I making a mess of the whole novel? That's the problem!

Imagine, I have already received several letters from various quarters congratulating me on the first part. This has greatly encouraged me. But, without wishing to flatter you, I must tell you directly that your response is worth more to me than anything. For a start, you don't just flatter me. Second, one brilliant observation stands out in your response: "These are *Turgenev's heroes in old age*." Brilliant! I had something like that in mind while I was writing, but you have summed it up in a pithy formula. Thank you for those words; you have shed light on the whole thing for me.

TO N. N. STRAKHOV, 18 (30) MAY 1871,
FROM DRESDEN

Dear Nikolai Nikolaevich, you began your letter directly with Belinsky after all. I anticipated this. But take a look at Paris, at the

Commune. Are you really one of those who say that once again it has failed through lack of people, circumstances, and so on? Throughout the whole of the nineteenth century this movement has either been dreaming of paradise on earth (beginning with the phalansteries), or, as soon as it begins to act (1848, 1849 – the present), it demonstrates a humiliating inability to say anything remotely positive. Essentially, it is all the same old Rousseau and the dream of changing the world on the basis of reason and experience (positivism). Surely, it would seem, there are already enough facts to suggest that their inability to say anything new is not fortuitous. They chop off heads, but why? Solely because this is easier than anything else. Actually saying something is incomparably harder. But desiring something is not the same as bringing it about. They desire the happiness of mankind, but they get no further than Rousseau's efforts to define the word *happiness*; that is, they get no further than an abstract idea not even justified by experience. The burning of Paris is a monstrosity: "We have not succeeded, therefore let the world go to ruin; for the Commune is higher than the happiness of the world and France." But, for them (and for many others), this rage is not a monstrosity but, on the contrary, a thing of beauty. In this way, the aesthetic sense has become confused in the new man. A moral basis for society that is derived from positivism not only fails to yield results, but it cannot even define itself, and it gets lost in aspirations and ideals. Are there really not enough facts by now to show that society is not constructed in that way and that such paths do not lead to happiness or bring about what they have imagined up to now? What will bring this about? They write many books, but they overlook the main thing: the West has lost Christ (because of Catholicism), and that is why the West is in a state of decline, the only reason. The ideal has changed, and how clear this is! The decline of papal authority alongside the decline of the leader of the Romano-Germanic world (France and friend) – what a coincidence!

All this demands lengthy and great discussion, but what I want to say is this: If Belinsky, Granovsky, and the whole of that riff-raff could see what is happening now, they would say: "No, that's not what we dreamed of; no, this is a deviation. Wait a little longer and the light will dawn, progress will triumph, and mankind will be restructured on sensible principles and will be happy!" No way would they agree that once that road has been taken, it can lead only to the Commune and Felix Piat.[15] They were so dim that even *now*, even after the event, they would not agree but would continue their dreaming. I have cursed Belinsky more as a phenomenon of Russian life than as a person. This was the most putrid, stupid, and shameful phenomenon of Russian life. There is one excuse – it was an inevitable phenomenon. And I assure you, Belinsky would have settled for the following idea: "Ah well, the Commune failed because, above all, it remained French, that is, it retained within itself the contagion of nationality. Therefore we must seek out a nation that does not retain a single drop of nationality and that is capable of beating its own mother about the face, like I have done with Russia." And, with mouth foaming, he would once again set about writing his foul articles, heaping shame on Russia, and denying its great phenomena (Pushkin), with the aim of finally turning Russia into a *vacant* nation capable of standing at the head of the cause of *mankind's universality* (*obshchechelovecheskogo dela*). He would happily accept the Jesuit outlook and falsehood of our progressive forces. But there is more: You never knew him, but I did. I saw it, and now I have come to understand him completely. That man once berated Christ to my face in the most obscene way, but he was never capable of setting himself and the world's other progressive forces alongside Christ for the sake of comparison. He was incapable of observing just how much petty vanity, malice, intolerance, irritability, baseness, and, above all, conceit there was in him and the others. In berating Christ, he never once asked himself: What shall we offer in his place? Surely not ourselves, given that we are so vile? No, it never crossed his mind that he might himself be vile. He was self-satisfied to the highest degree, and that was stupidity of the most individual, putrid, and shameful kind. You say he was talented. Quite the contrary . . .

TO N. A. LIUBIMOV, MARCH—APRIL 1872,
FROM PETERSBURG[16]

It seems to me that what I have sent you (the first chapter "At Tikhon's," three small chapters) can now be published. All that is really scabrous has been excised, while what is most important has been preserved. The whole of that half-insane outburst is sufficiently revealed, although it will be revealed more forcefully later. I swear to you, I could not help but retain the essentials of the matter. This is an entire social type (in my firm view), one of *our* Russian types, the sort of empty man who is empty not by choice, but because he has lost his ties to everything native, and most of all to his faith. He is depraved *out of anguish*, but he has a conscience and resorts to convulsive efforts that are full of suffering in order to renew himself and start to believe once more. Along with the nihilists this is a serious phenomenon, and one that I swear exists in reality. This is a man who cannot believe in the faith of our believers, but who demands total and complete faith, otherwise. . . . But everything will become clearer in part 3.

TO A. A. ROMANOV (HEIR TO THE THRONE),
10 FEBRUARY 1873, FROM PETERSBURG[17]

Your Imperial Highness, Sire,

Allow me the honor and happiness of presenting my work for your attention. It is almost a historical sketch, by means of which I wanted to explain how such monstrous phenomena as the Nechaev crime are possible in our strange society. My view is that these phenomena are not fortuitous and are not isolated instances, and, for this reason, neither the events nor the characters in my novel are exact copies. These phenomena are the direct consequence of the long alienation of Russian culture from the native, original principles of Russian life. Even the most gifted representatives of our pseudo-European development have long since concluded that it is completely criminal for us Russians even to dream of our own originality. Most terrible of all is that they are quite right, for once we have *proudly* proclaimed ourselves Europeans, we cease to be Russians. Confused and fearful at the extent to which we have fallen behind Europe in intellectual and scientific development, we have forgotten that we ourselves, in the profundity and mission of our Russian spirit, perhaps possess, by virtue of being Russian, the capacity to bring new light to the world because of the originality of our development. We are so taken up by our own degradation that we have forgotten that most immutable of all historical laws, the one stating that without such an *arrogant* view of our own world significance as a nation, we can never be a great nation that will leave something uniquely its own for the benefit of the whole of mankind. We have forgotten that all the great nations gave expression to their forces of greatness through this kind of *arrogant* self-regard and that they brought benefit to the world, each of them introducing at least one ray of light, by virtue of the fact that they remained themselves: proud, steadfast, and forever *arrogantly* independent.

To think like this in our country today, and to utter such thoughts, is to brand oneself a pariah. But, meanwhile, the most outstanding proponents of our lack of national originality would be the first to turn away in horror from the Nechaev business. Our Belinskys and Granovskys would not have believed it had they been told that they were the direct progenitors of Nechaev. It is precisely this kindredship and continuity of thought, developing from fathers to children, that I wished to express in my work. I am far from having succeeded entirely, but I have done my best.

I am flattered, and my spirit is lifted, by the hope that you, Sire, the heir to one of the most sublime and serious destinies in the world, the future leader and ruler of the Russian land, will perhaps pay some small heed to my attempt – weak, I know, but conscientious – to depict in artistic form one of the most dangerous ulcers in our present civilized class, a civilized class that is strange, unnatural, and unoriginal but that still remains at the forefront of our Russian life.

Allow me, Sire, to remain with feelings of unbounded respect and gratitude your most obedient and devoted servant,
Fedor Dostoevsky

NOTES

All translations are by W. J. Leatherbarrow from texts in *PSS*, 29/i.

1. For letters written from abroad, two dates of composition are given. The first is according to the Julian calendar used in Russia until 31 January 1918, and the second (in parentheses) is according to the Gregorian calendar used in the West. Letters written from Russia are dated according to the Julian calendar.

2. The book referred to is A. V. Stankevich, *Timofei Nikolaevich Granovskii: biograficheskii ocherk* (Moscow: n.p., 1869).

3. Here, Dostoevsky is referring to his work on *The Life of a Great Sinner.*

4. A galley page (or printer's page) is the equivalent of sixteen book pages.

5. V. V. Kashpirev was the editor of the periodical *Zaria* (Dawn).

6. Tikhon Zadonsky was an eighteenth-century clergyman and writer who was sanctified in 1860.

7. P. Ia. Chaadaev (1793–1856) was the author of *Philosophical Letters,* the first of which was published in 1836, creating a furor with its uncompromising criticism of Russian historical, cultural, and religious isolation from Western Europe.

8. A character from the second part of Gogol's *Dead Souls* (1842).

9. Andrei Stolz, whose Westernized practicality is offered as a counterbalance to Oblomov's indigenous idleness.

10. Characters from Chernyshevsky's novel *What Is to Be Done?* (1863).

11. A. A. Kraevsky was the editor of the periodical *Otechestvennye zapiski* (Notes of the fatherland). Although Kraevsky had been Dostoevsky's editor, relations between the two had become strained.

12. A. Serno-Solovevich was a radical of the younger generation, renowned for his dismissal of Herzen as a washed-out liberal of the past.

13. A. N. Pleshcheev (1825–1893) was a poet and friend of Dostoevsky in the Petrashevsky circle.

14. P. V. Annenkov (1812–1887) was a critic and memoirist, best known for his account of the early Westernizers, including Belinsky and Herzen, in

The Extraordinary Decade, translated by I. R. Titunik (Ann Arbor: University of Michigan Press, 1968).

15. Felix Piat (1810–1889) was a committee member of the Paris Commune of 1871 and an advocate of terror.

16. N. A. Liubimov was associate editor at *Russkii vestnik* (The Russian Herald).

17. The letter is addressed to the future Alexander III, and it accompanied a copy of the separate edition of *The Devils*, which had appeared earlier that year.

IV   SELECT BIBLIOGRAPHY

This bibliography contains a selection of the most important works on *The Devils* in English and Russian, as well as the most relevant general studies of Dostoevsky. It does not include all material cited in the notes to the essays. For a more complete annotated bibliography, as well as a guide to other bibliographic sources, see W. J. Leatherbarrow, *Fedor Dostoevsky: A Reference Guide*, cited below.

Alexandrov, Vladimir E. "The Narrator as Author in Dostoevskij's *Besy.*" *Russian Literature* 15 (1984): 243–54. Discusses narrative inconsistencies in the novel.

Bakhtin, M. M. *Problems of Dostoevsky's Poetics*, edited and translated by Caryl Emerson. Manchester: Manchester University Press, 1984. Fundamental study of narrative polyphony and carnivalization as basic principles of Dostoevsky's art.

Batiuto, A. I. "Idei i obrazy: k probleme 'I.S. Turgenev i F.M. Dostoevskii v 1860–70e gody'" [Ideas and images: On the problem of I. S. Turgenev and F. M. Dostoevsky in the 1860s and 1870s]. *Russkaia literatura*, no. 1 (1982): 76–96.

Belknap, Robert. "Shakespeare and *The Possessed.*" *Dostoevsky Studies* 5 (1984): 63–69.

Berdyaev, Nicholas. *Dostoevsky*, translated by Donald Attwater. New York: New American Library, 1974. Classic study of religious and philosophical dimensions of Dostoevsky's works.

Blackmur, R. P. "In the Birdcage. Notes on *The Possessed* of Dostoevsky." In *Eleven Essays in the European Novel*, 163–84. New York: Harcourt, Brace & World, 1964. Relates the politics of the novel to its metaphysical themes.

Boertnes, Jostein. "The Last Delusion in an Infinite Series of Delusions: Stavrogin and the Symbolic Structure of *The Devils.*" *Dostoevsky Studies* 4 (1983): 53–67.

Budanova, N. F. "O nekotorykh istochnikakh nravstvenno-filosofskoi problematiki romana *Besy*" [Some sources of the moral and philosophical content of *The Devils*]. In *Dostoevskii: Materialy i issledovaniia*, vol. 8, edited by G. M. Fridlender, 93–106. Leningrad: Nauka, 1988. On the influence of old Russian sources on the chapter "At Tikhon's."

———. "Problema 'ottsov i detei' v romane *Besy*" [The problem of "fathers and sons" in *The Devils*]. In *Dostoevskii: Materialy i issledovaniia*, vol. 1, edited by G. M. Fridlender, 164–88.

Leningrad: Nauka, 1974. On the significance of Turgenev in the novel's ideological design.

Busch, R. L. *Humor in the Major Novels of Dostoevsky.* Columbus, Ohio: Slavica, 1987.

———. "Turgenev's *Ottsy i deti* and Dostoevskii's *Besy.*" *Canadian Slavonic Papers* 26 (1984): 1–9. Compares treatments of the theme of generational conflict.

Camus, Albert. *The Myth of Sisyphus and Other Essays,* translated by Justin O'Brien. New York: Knopf, 1955. Concentrates on the suicide of Kirillov and on those aspects of *The Devils* that distinguish Dostoevsky as an "existentialist" writer.

Catteau, Jacques. "Le Christ dans le miroir des grotesques (*Les Démons*)." *Dostoevsky Studies* 4 (1983): 29–36. Analyzes Stavrogin, Kirillov, and Peter Verkhovensky as travesties of Christ.

———. *Dostoyevsky and the Process of Literary Creation,* translated by Audrey Littlewood. Cambridge: Cambridge University Press, 1989. Detailed treatment of the creative processes behind Dostoevsky's novels.

Cerny, Vaclav. *Dostoevsky and His Devils,* translated by F. W. Galan. Ann Arbor, Mich.: Ardis, 1975. Argues that Dostoevsky's talents as a polemicist outstrip his talents as an artist, and emphasizes the cruel and sadistic aspects of his art.

Chapple, Richard A. *A Dostoevsky Dictionary.* Ann Arbor, Mich.: Ardis, 1983.

Coetzee, J. M. *The Master of Petersburg.* London: Secker & Warburg, 1994. Interesting, if historically unreliable, fictional account of the period in Dostoevsky's life when he was working on *The Devils.*

Cox, Gary. "Stavrogin and Prince Hal." *Canadian Slavonic Papers* 26 (1984): 121–26.

Danow, David K. "Stavrogin's Teachings: Reported Speech in *The Possessed.*" *Slavic and East European Journal* 32 (1988): 213–24. A Bakhtinian reading showing how Stavrogin's "word" is appropriated by other characters.

Davison, R. M. "Aspects of Novelistic Technique in Dostoevskii's *Besy.*" In *From Pushkin to "Palisandriia": Essays on the Russian Novel in Honor of Richard Freeborn,* edited by A. McMillin, 83–95. New York: St. Martin's, 1990.

———. "*The Devils:* The Role of Stavrogin." In *New Essays on Dostoyevsky,* edited by Malcolm V. Jones and Garth M. Terry, 95–114. Cambridge: Cambridge University Press, 1983.

———. "Dostoevsky's *Devils* and the Sects." *Die Welt der Slaven* 26 (1981): 274–84. On Russian religious sectarianism in the novel.

Dolinin, A. S. F. M. *Dostoevskii v vospominaniiakh sovremennikov* [F. M. Dostoevsky in the Recollections of His Contemporaries]. 2 vols. Moscow: Khudozhestvennaia literatura, 1964.

—————. "Ispoved' Stavrogina (v sviazi s kompozitsiei *Besov*)" [Stavrogin's confession and the composition of *The Devils*]. *Literaturnaia mysl'*, no. 1 (1922), 139–62. An early, but still valuable discussion of the "banned chapter" and its function in the novel.

—————. "Turgenev v *Besakh*" [Turgenev in *The Devils*]. In F. M. *Dostoevskii: Stat'i i materialy*, vol. 2, 119–36. Leningrad: Mysl', 1924. Still the finest treatment of the theme.

Dostoevskaia, A. G. *Vospominaniia* [Memoirs]. Moscow: Khudozhestvennaia literatura, 1971. The memoirs of Dostoevsky's second wife.

Dowler, Wayne. *Dostoevsky, Grigor'ev, and Native Soil Conservatism.* Toronto: University of Toronto Press, 1982. A full account of Dostoevsky's nationalist views.

Ermakova, M. Ia. "Dvoinichestvo v *Besakh*" [Dualism in *The Devils*]. In *Dostoevskii: Materialy i issledovaniia*, vol. 2, edited by G. M. Fridlender, 113–18. Leningrad: Nauka, 1976.

Evnin, F. I. "Roman *Besy*" [The novel *The Devils*]. In *Tvorchestvo F. M. Dostoevskogo*, edited by N. L. Stepanov, D. D. Blagoi, U. A. Gural'nik, and B. S. Riurikov, 215–64. Moscow: Izd. Akademiia nauk SSSR, 1959. A comprehensive introduction to the novel.

Fanger, Donald. *Dostoevsky and Romantic Realism: A Study of Dostoevsky in Relation to Balzac, Dickens, and Gogol.* Cambridge, Mass.: Harvard University Press, 1965.

Fitzgerald, G. D. "Anton Lavrent'evic G——v: The Narrator as Re-creator in Dostoevskij's *The Possessed*." In *New Perspectives on Nineteenth-Century Russian Prose*, edited by G. J. Gutsche and L. G. Leighton, 121–34. Columbus, Ohio: Slavica, 1982.

—————. "The Chronology of F. M. Dostoevskij's *The Possessed*." *Slavic and East European Journal* 27 (1983): 19–46. Tests the claim of the narrator to be a chronicler by reconstructing the sequence of events on the basis of textual clues.

Frank, Joseph. *Dostoevsky: The Seeds of Revolt, 1821–1849.* Princeton, N.J.: Princeton University Press, 1976. First volume of the finest literary biography of Dostoevsky.

—————. *Dostoevsky: The Years of Ordeal, 1850–1859.* Princeton, N.J.: Princeton University Press, 1983.

—————. *Dostoevsky: The Stir of Liberation, 1860–1865.* Princeton, N.J.: Princeton University Press, 1986.

—————. *Dostoevsky: The Miraculous Years, 1865–1871.* Princeton, N.J.:

Princeton University Press, 1995. The volume of Frank's biography that deals with the textual and contextual analysis of *The Devils*.

———. "The Masks of Stavrogin." *Sewanee Review* 77 (1969): 660–91. On the thematic and compositional centrality of Stavrogin.

Fuchs, Ina. *Die Herausforderung des Nihilismus: Philosophische Analysen zu F. M. Dostoevskijs Werk "Die Dämonen."* Munich: Otto Sagner, 1987. An application of philosophical interpretations of nihilism to Dostoevsky's text.

Fusso, Susanne. "Maidens in Childbirth: The Sistine Madonna in Dostoevskii's *Devils.*" *Slavic Review* 54 (1995): 261–75.

Gregory, S. V. "Dostoevskii's *The Devils* and the Anti-Nihilist Novel." *Slavic Review* 38 (1979): 444–55.

Grossman, L. P. "Stilistika Stavrogina" [Stavrogin's stylistics]. In *F. M. Dostoevskii: Stat'i i materialy*, vol. 2, edited by A. S. Dolinin, 139–48. Leningrad: Mysl', 1924. Discusses Stavrogin's use of language and relates his interview with Tikhon to the literary genre of the confession.

Grossman, L. P., and V. P. Polonskii. *Spor o Bakunine i Dostoevskom* [The controversy over Bakunin and Dostoevsky]. Leningrad: GIZ, 1926. Rehearses arguments for and against Bakunin as a prototype of Stavrogin.

Holquist, J. M. *Dostoevsky and the Novel*. Princeton, N.J.: Princeton University Press, 1977. Contains an interesting treatment of time in Dostoevsky's novels.

Howe, Irving. "Dostoevsky: The Politics of Salvation." In *Politics and the Novel*, 51–75. New York: Horizon Press, 1957. A classic essay discussing the relationship of *The Devils* to the sociopolitical currents of its age.

Ivanov, Vyacheslav. *Freedom and the Tragic Life: A Study in Dostoevsky*, translated by Norman Cameron. Wolfeboro, N.H.: Longwood Academic, 1989.

Jackson, Robert Louis. *Dostoevsky's Quest for Form: A Study of His Philosophy of Art*. Bloomington, Ind.: Physsardt, 1978. A fine study of Dostoevsky's aesthetic views.

Jones, John. *Dostoevsky*. Oxford: Clarendon, 1983. Discusses authorial and narrative strategies in Dostoevsky's works.

Jones, Malcolm V. *Dostoyevsky after Bakhtin: Readings in Dostoyevsky's Fantastic Realism*. Cambridge: Cambridge University Press, 1990. A very accessible application of literary theory.

———. *Dostoyevsky: The Novel of Discord*. London: Paul Elek, 1976. Concentrates on the characteristics of disorder, travesty, and discord in the narrative tactics of Dostoevsky's novels.

Kariakin, Iu. F. "Zachem khroniker v *Besakh?*" [Why a chronicler in *The Devils?*]. In *Dostoevskii: Materialy i issledovaniia*, vol. 5, edited by G. M. Fridlender, 113–31. Leningrad: Nauka, 1983.

Kiraly, Gyula. "To the Question of Subject Composition and Poetic Motifs in *The Devils:* The Function of Stavrogin and Verkhovensky in the Novel." *Acta litteraria academiae scientiarum hungaricae* 28, nos. 1–2 (1986): 91–118.

Kjetsaa, Geir. *Dostoevsky and His New Testament*. Atlantic Highlands, N.J.: Humanities Press, 1984. An analysis of the annotations in Dostoevsky's New Testament.

―――. *Fyodor Dostoevsky: A Writer's Life*. London: Macmillan, 1988.

Kogan, G. F. "Iz istorii sozdaniia 'Ispovedi Stavrogina'" [From the compositional history of "Stavrogin's Confession"]. *Izvestiia Akademii nauk SSSR: Seriia literatury i iazyka* 54, no. 1 (1995): 65–73.

Kohn, Hans. "Dostoyevsky and Danilevsky: Nationalist Messianism." In *Continuity and Change in Russian and Soviet Thought*, edited by E. J. Simmons, 500–515. Cambridge, Mass.: Harvard University Press, 1955. On Dostoevsky's anti-Westernism and his views on Russia's destiny.

Kovsan, M. L. "Khudozhestvennoe vremia v romane F. M. Dostoevskogo *Besy*" [Artistic time in *The Devils*]. *Filologicheskie nauki*, no. 5 (1982): 24–30. On the relationship between historical and subjectively perceived time in *The Devils*.

Leatherbarrow, W. J. "Apocalyptic Imagery in *The Idiot* and *The Devils*." *Dostoevsky Studies* 3 (1982): 43–52.

―――. *Fedor Dostoevsky*. Boston: Twayne, 1981.

―――. *Fedor Dostoevsky: A Reference Guide*. Boston: G. K. Hall, 1990.

Linnér, Sven. "Bishop Tichon in *The Possessed*." *Russian Literature* 4 (1976): 273–84.

―――. *Dostoevskij on Realism*. Stockholm: Almqvist & Wiksell, 1962. A useful collection of Dostoevsky's statements on art.

Livermore, Gordon. "Stepan Verkhovensky and the Shaping Dialectic of Dostoevsky's *Devils*." In *Dostoevsky: New Perspectives*, edited by Robert Louis Jackson, 176–92. Englewood Cliffs, N.J.: Prentice Hall, 1984. Explores Dostoevsky's attitude to the idealism represented by Stepan Trofimovich.

Loginovskaia, E. "Motiv demonizma v *Besakh* Dostoevskogo: Tekstovye i vnetekstovye koordinaty" [The motif of demonism in *The Devils*: Textual and extra-textual coordinates]. *Scando-Slavica* 26 (1981): 33–52. Explores *The Devils* as a polemical engagement with Lermontov and Gogol.

Mann, R. "The Faustian Pattern in *The Devils*." *Canadian Slavonic*

Papers 24 (1982): 239–44. On echoes of Goethe's *Faust* in the structural and thematic features of *The Devils*.

Matlaw, Ralph E. "The Chronicler of *The Possessed*: Character and Function." *Dostoevsky Studies* 5 (1984): 37–47.

Meijer, Jan. "Some Remarks on Dostoevskij's *Besy*." In *Dutch Contributions to the Fifth International Congress of Slavicists, Sofia, 1963*, 125–44. The Hague: Mouton, 1963. On disparities between Dostoevsky's ideological intentions and how these were realized in the novel.

Merrill, Reed. "The Demon of Irony: Stavrogin the Adversary at Tikhon's." In *Dostoevski and the Human Condition after a Century*, edited by A. Ugrinsky, F. S. Lambasa, and V. K. Ozolins, 87–97. Westport, Conn.: Greenwood, 1986. Bakhtinian analysis of the dialectics of the chapter "At Tikhon's."

Miller, Robin Feuer. "Imitations of Rousseau in *The Possessed*." *Dostoevsky Studies* 5 (1984): 77–89. On resemblances between Stepan Trofimovich Verkhovensky and Rousseau.

Mochulsky, Konstantin. *Dostoevsky: His Life and Work*, translated by M. Minihan. Princeton, N.J.: Princeton University Press, 1973. Still the best general biographical-critical study of Dostoevsky.

Mondry, Henrietta. "Another Literary Parody in *The Possessed*." In *Dostoevsky and the Twentieth Century: The Ljubljana Papers*, edited by Malcolm V. Jones, 277–88. Nottingham: Astra, 1993. Suggests that Stepan Trofimovich Verkhovensky is a parody of Tolstoy.

Moore, G. M. "The Voices of Legion: The Narrator of *The Possessed*." *Dostoevsky Studies* 6 (1985): 51–66.

Morch, Audun J. "Dostoevskij's *Besy*: Revolutionaries with Speech Deficiency." *Scando-Slavica* 39 (1993): 62–73.

Moser, Charles A. *Antinihilism in the Russian Novel of the 1860s*. The Hague: Mouton, 1964. Provides a useful context for understanding *The Devils* as a polemical novel.

———. "Stepan Trofimovic Verkhovenskij and the Esthetics of His Time." *Slavic and East European Journal* 29 (1985): 157–63.

———. "Svidrigailov and Stavrogin." *Forum International* (German and Slavic Department, University of Maryland) 3 (1980): 88–98. Argues that Stavrogin is a fuller development of Dostoevsky's polemic against the rational ethic of the men of the 1860s begun in the figure of Svidrigailov in *Crime and Punishment*.

Murav, Harriet. "Representations of the Demonic: Seventeenth-Century Pretenders and *The Devils*." *Slavic and East European Journal* 35 (1991): 56–70. Shows how Russian historico-cultural motifs are embedded in *The Devils*.

Natov, Nadine. "Rol' filosofskogo podteksta v romane *Besy*" [The role of the philosophical subtext in *The Devils*]. In *Zapiski russkoi akademicheskoi gruppy v SShA* [Transactions of the Association of Russian-American Scholars in the USA] 14 (1981): 69–100. Traces direct and indirect philosophical citation in *The Devils*.

———. "The Theme of 'Chantage' (Blackmail) in *The Possessed*: Art and Reality." *Dostoevsky Studies* 6 (1985): 3–33.

Oates, Joyce Carol. "Tragic Rites in Dostoyevsky's *The Possessed*." In *Contraries: Essays*, 17–50. New York: Oxford University Press, 1981. Shows how the novel emerges from a mythic, rather than realistic, imagination.

Ozolins, V. K. "The Concept of Beauty in *The Possessed*." In *Dostoevski and the Human Condition after a Century*, edited by A Ugrinsky, F. S. Lambasa, and V. K. Ozolins, 99–111. Westport, Conn.: Greenwood, 1986. Relates Stepan Trofimovich's aesthetic views to those of Dostoevsky himself.

Peace, Richard. *Dostoyevsky: An Examination of the Major Novels*. Cambridge: Cambridge University Press, 1971. Offers a close reading of *The Devils*, interpreting the novel's symbolism and exploring the importance of religious sectarianism.

Pomper, Philip. *Sergei Nechaev*. New Brunswick, N.J.: Rutgers University Press, 1979. A study of the political figure who served as a model for Peter Verkhovensky.

Pope, Richard. "Peter Verkhovensky and the Banality of Evil." In *Dostoevsky and the Twentieth Century: The Ljubljana Papers*, edited by Malcolm V. Jones, 39–48. Nottingham: Astra, 1993.

Pope, Richard, and Judy Turner. "Toward Understanding Stavrogin." *Slavic Review* 49 (1990): 543–53.

Rahv, Philip. "Dostoevski in *The Possessed*." In *Essays on Literature and Politics, 1932–1972*, 107–28. Boston: Houghton Mifflin, 1978. Discusses the political dimension and implications of the novel.

Rzhevsky, Leonid. "Dostoevskij's *Besy*: Its Language and the Author's Image." *Russian Language Journal* 34, no. 117 (1980): 101–8.

Saraskina, Liudmila. *Besy: Roman-preduprezhdenie* [*The Devils*: A novel-warning]. Moscow: Sovetskii pisatel', 1990. On the prophetic qualities on the novel.

Serman, I. Z. "Stikhi Kapitana Lebiadkina i poeziia XX veka" [Captain Lebiadkin's verses and twentieth-century poetry]. *Revue des études slaves* 53 (1981): 597–605. Argues that Lebiadkin's verses should be taken more seriously in their anticipation of modern literary absurdism.

Slattery, D. P. "Idols and Icons: Comic Transformation in

Dostoevsky's *The Possessed.*" *Dostoevsky Studies* 6 (1985): 35–50. Considers the symbolic role of the icon and its contribution to the novel's carnival spirit.

Smith, J. "Stavrogin's Confession and Religious Existentialism." *University of Dayton Review* 18, no. 3 (1987): 37–47.

Steiner, George. *Tolstoy or Dostoevsky? An Essay in the Old Criticism.* New York: Vintage, 1959. Classic study of Dostoevsky as a "dramatic" novelist.

Stenbock-Fermor, Elizabeth. "Lermontov and Dostoevskij's Novel *The Devils.*" *Slavic and East European Journal* 17 (new style 3) (1959): 215–30. On Stavrogin, Pechorin, and the literary-cultural phenomenon of the Byronic hero.

———. "Stavrogin's Quest in *The Devils* of Dostoevskij." In *To Honor Roman Jakobson: Essays on the Occasion of His Seventieth Birthday, 11 October 1966*, vol. 3, 1926–34. The Hague and Paris: Mouton, 1967.

Tunimanov, V. A. "Rasskazchik v *Besakh* Dostoevskogo" [The narrator in *The Devils*]. In *Issledovaniia po poetike i stilistike*, edited by V. V. Vinogradov, 87–162. Leningrad: Nauka, 1972. Extract in English in *Dostoevsky: New Perspectives*, edited by Robert Louis Jackson, 145–75. Englewood Cliffs, N.J.: Prentice-Hall, 1984. Clarifies the elusive role of the narrator to argue that *The Devils* is one of the most carefully contructed of Dostoevsky's novels.

Vladiv, S. V. *Narrative Principles in Dostoevskij's "Besy": A Structural Analysis.* Berne: Peter Lang, 1979. The most detailed treatment of the narrative persona employed by Dostoevsky in *The Devils*.

Ward, Bruce K. *Dostoyevsky's Critique of the West: The Quest for Earthly Paradise.* Waterloo, Ontario: Wilfried Laurier University Press, 1988.

Wasiolek, Edward, ed. *Dostoevsky: The Major Fiction.* Cambridge, Mass.: MIT Press, 1964.

———. *Fyodor Dostoevsky: The Notebooks for "The Possessed,"* translated by Victor Terras. Chicago: University of Chicago Press, 1968. Wasiolek's introduction also provides a coherent account of the novel's complex evolution.

Contributors

R. M. Davison was a lecturer in Russian at the University of Liverpool, England, until his retirement. He has written many articles on Dostoevsky.

M. V. Jones is Emeritus Professor of Russian at the University of Nottingham, England, and a former president of the International Dostoevsky Society. He is the author of many articles and books on Dostoevsky, the most recent of which, *Dostoyevsky after Bakhtin* (1990), has also appeared in a Russian edition. He is also editor, with Robin Feuer Miller, of *The Cambridge Companion to the Classic Russian Novel* (1998).

W. J. Leatherbarrow is Professor of Russian at the University of Sheffield, England. He is the author of several works on Dostoevsky, the most recent of which are *Fedor Dostoevsky: A Reference Guide* (1990); *Dostoyevsky's The Brothers Karamazov* (1992); and *Dostoevskii and Britain* (1995). He is also co-editor, with D. C. Offord, of *A Documentary History of Russian Thought* (1987).

D. C. Offord is Professor of Russian at the University of Bristol, England. He is well known as a historian of ideas in Russia and has written books on Russian liberalism and Russian populism. He has also written essays on Dostoevsky's polemical relationship with the Russian radicals of the 1860s.